Tools of the Cowboy Trade

Saddle by Monte Beckman; bit by Ernie Marsh; headstall by Mark Dahl; spurs by Jeremiah Watt Productions; quirt by Casey Backus; reins and reata by Alfredo Campos.

Tools of the Cowboy Trade

Today's Crafters of Saddles, Bits, Spurs and Trappings

Casey Beard

Photographs by

Dale DeGabriele

SALT LAKE CITY

To the ennobling spirit of the West, the enduring creativity of the artisan, and my wife, Anne, who embodies both. She is a true partner on life's trail.

First edition

99 98 97   3 2 1

This is a Peregrine Smith Book, published by
Gibbs Smith, Publisher
P.O. Box 667
Layton, Utah 84041

Design by J. Scott Knudsen, Park City, Utah
Printed and bound in Korea

On the front cover: bit by the Hayes family
On the back cover: saddle by Dale Harwood

Library of Congress Cataloging-in-Publication Data
Beard, Casey, 1948–
Tools of the cowboy trade : today's crafters of saddles, bits, spurs and trappings / Casey Beard : photographs by Dale DeGabriele.
p. cm.
ISBN 0-87905-732-7
1. Saddlery—United States. 2. Leather workers—United States. 3. Cowboys—United States. I. DeGabriele, Dale, 1952– . II. Title.
TS1032.B38 1996
685'.1'0973—dc20   95-42171
CIP

Contents

ACKNOWLEDGMENTS

It takes a lot of hands to get a project like this into the catch pen. Without the generosity and help of many people, this book would still be wandering in the back forty of the author's mind. Dale and I are deeply indebted to the following people and organizations who helped us gather up and deliver *Tools of the Cowboy Trade:*

Roger Allgeier, Don King, Gary Dunshee, the Trappings of the American West staff, Loren and Margaret Wood, the Currin Family, Clint Johnson, Dary Reed, Vicky Mullins, Dave and Linda Lundy, the Anderson Family, Randy Hoffman and Nicole Hoffman, Winston Bruce, Mike and Dene Hosker, the PRCA, the Sisters Rodeo, the Pendleton Round-Up, the Farm-City Pro Rodeo, Clint Corey, Larry Sandvick, Andy Ely, Randy Allen, Butch Knowles, the Roberts Family, Jane Glennie-Carlson, Mike and Diana Hopper and Frank and Charlot Beard. Special recognition is due Doubleday, Bantam, Dell Publishing for their kind permission to reprint portions of Charlie Russell's *Trails Plowed Under,* © 1927. Finally, we are indebted to Madge Baird for her commitment to and belief in this project.

Tools of the Cowboy Trade

The appreciation of fine cowboy gear reaches far beyond the ranges where cowboys still ply their trade. Saddles, bits and spurs can be found on spreads in Manhattan and Beverly Hills where the "little doggies" are named Fifi or Pierre.

The broad appeal of trappings reflects the hold the cowboy retains on the nation's psyche, embodying our collective self-image. Radically transformed by the onslaught of new technologies, other callings associated with settling the West—hard-rock mining, lumberjacking, farming and railroading—have faded in the nation's consciousness. Cowboying, however, endures little changed. As a cultural agent, the cowboy has enriched our civilization, spawning a vibrant vernacular vocabulary, distinctive costume, school of literature, body of poetry, and unique music and dance forms. This contribution to our folkways is truly remarkable. In large measure, this explains the enduring appeal of western gear. The cowboy's saddle, bit, spurs and trappings are coveted for their intrinsic design values, craftsmanship and testament to a revered way of life.

Historically, the American cowboy was a species new to the world, an egalitarian nobility beholden to no man. Though often of humble origins, a well-mounted cowboy felt the equal of anyone and pitied those who earned a living afoot. As someone once observed, "The world looks different from the back of a horse."

Cowboying is the quintessential American trade. Rich with the heritage of Spain—*chaparejos* or chaps, lariat, latigo, mecate, quirt, reata and tapaderos—its tools are now uniquely American. Produced in the crucible of post-Civil War America, the ranks of the cowboy fraternity included displaced Southern veterans, Yankee adventurers, Hispanic vaqueros, freed slaves, Native Americans and emigrants fresh from Europe. No other occupation has been so encompassing, so representative of the great melting pot. It remains a trade where a man's ability and character are what count. With his code of stoic endurance, self-reliance, loyalty, courage, camaraderie and pride in his skills, this knight of the western plains captured the nation's imagination, a hold retained to this day.

Tangible manifestations of a way of life, the trappings of the cowboy's trade are cultural icons. Symbols creating a sense of time and place, bits, spurs and saddles share a common heritage whether they ornament a New York penthouse or hang on a Nevada buckaroo's tack-room wall.

Charlie Russell recognized the interplay between the practical utility and ornamental qualities of a cowhand's rig. Gifted with pen as well as paintbrush, he captured this relationship in "The Story of the Cowpuncher," from his classic book *Trails Plowed Under.* Speaking of the cowboy's origins, his narrator, Rawhide Rawlins, relates:

> Texas an' California, bein' the startin' places, made two species of cowpunchers: those west of the Rockies rangin' north, usin' centerfire or single-cinch saddles, with high fork an' cantle; packed a sixty or sixty-five foot rawhide rope, an' swung a big loop. These cow people were generally strong on pretty, usin' plenty of hoss jewelry, silver mounted spurs, bits, an' conchos; instead of a quirt, used a romel, or quirt braided to the end of the reins. Their saddles were full stamped, with from twenty-four to twenty-eight inch eagle-billed tapaderos. Their chaparejos were made of fur or hair, either bear, angora goat or hair sealskin. These fellows were sure fancy, an' called themselves buccaroos, coming from the Spanish word, vaquero.
>
> The cowpuncher east of the Rockies originated in Texas and ranged north to the Big Bow. He wasn't much for pretty; his saddle was low horn, rimfire, or double-cinch; sometimes "macheer." Their rope was seldom over forty feet, for being a good deal in a brush country, they were forced to swing a small loop. These men generally tied, instead of taking their dallie-welts, or wrapping their rope around the saddle horn. Their chaparejos were made of heavy bullhide, to protect the legs from brush an' thorns, with hog snout tapaderos.
>
> Cowpunchers were mighty particular about their rig, an' in all the camps you'd find a fashion leader. From a cowpuncher's idea, these fellers was sure good to look at, an' I tell you right now, there ain't no prettier sight for my eyes than one of those good-lookin', long-backed cowpunchers, sittin' up on a high-forked, full-stamped California saddle with a live hoss between his legs.

To service the burgeoning post-Civil War demand for cowboy gear, enterprising craftsmen set up shop to produce saddles, bits, spurs and tack. Handy waddies and buckaroos making their own gear gained a bunkhouse following that spread to other ranches in an area. Blacksmiths and leather workers plying their trade in the rough and tumble cow towns dotting the West saw opportunity firsthand. Newly arrived immigrants, schooled in the trades of harness making and metalwork back in the Old Country, saw gear making as the path leading to America's streets of gold. In those early days, regionalism was rampant, innovation constant and competition fierce. While most remained cottage industries, some suppliers developed into major manufacturing enterprises, often far removed from their client's stomping grounds west of the Mississippi. The August Bueurmann Manufacturing Company, a major producer of bits and spurs, was located in Newark, New Jersey.

Some makers were so successful that their name and product became synonymous. In the southwest, spurs were often called "Kelly's" in recognition of P. M. Kelly and Sons of El Paso, Texas. Typical of most leading gear makers, the Kellys lived in cow country and incorporated actual experience in the design of their bits and spurs. Over time, certain brands and names emerged as favorites among working cowboys. Saddles made by Porter, Visalia, Collins, Lawrence, Meanea, Hamley and Cogshall were instantly recognized in cowboy circles. Similarly, Garcia, McChesney, Kelly, Morales and Crockett meant fine-quality bits and spurs.

Dozens of books have been penned about this old-time gear. Collecting vintage western memorabilia is a popular hobby. Old saddles, bits, spurs and related trappings fetch prices at auction that would leave their makers and the waddies and buckaroos who used them dumbfounded. Functional beauty, quality workmanship and historical significance contribute to the enduring popularity of these antiques. Cowboy collectables do not, however, celebrate a lost, arcane way of life. Fascination with vintage gear coincides with a renaissance in contemporary cowboy crafts. As vintage gear is hammered down at ever-higher prices and quality pieces become scarcer, many collectors are turning their attention to the work of leading contemporary makers. Those aficionados who have switched their passion to today's gear are able to choose from a cornucopia of masterworks.

As in Rawhide Rawlins' day, the cowboy fraternity remains a fashion-conscious lot. They prize stylish, well-made, eye-catching gear that sets them apart from their fellows. From Mexico to the Big Bow River of the North, and from where the trees get scarce in the East to the old Pacific, talented, dedicated craftsmen continue to create exceptional tools of the trade for contemporary working cowboys.

A latter-day artisans guild, they are a brotherhood of master craftsmen toiling away in small workshops across the West. Like itinerant medieval journeymen, many wander from place to place, practicing their trade across the West's vast reaches. Others labor at the benches where they learned their craft from their fathers, as their fathers did before them. Some work in splendid isolation while others share their days with family members or apprentices. True artisans, their love of the craft is as important as its

At the Farm City Pro Rodeo, horsewoman Diana Hopper sports a pair of Hayes spurs.

financial rewards. With their talents, all could make more money, work less and face fewer tribulations by surrendering to mass production's temptations or abandoning the trade for more lucrative employment. If the Bureau of Labor Standards required craftsmen to pay themselves minimum wage and provide the benefits most workers take for granted, they would have to shut themselves down.

Whether working in leather, steel, rawhide, horsehair or silver, these artisans share a passion for their craft, reverence for the traditions they perpetuate and total commitment to the western way of life. Blessed with technical mastery and artistic flair, each strives for perfection. In an increasingly impersonal, homogeneous world, they refuse to compromise with mediocrity and conformity. When they put their mark on a saddle, bit or pair of spurs, it is a mark of excellence. Many craftspeople take offense at the term "functional art," regarding it as pejorative. In contrast, cowboy craftsmen take offense if their work is not considered functional. Their goal is to make working tools that are also beautiful. In this, they share many ideals of the Arts and Crafts movement that flourished earlier this century. Their work is part of a philosophy of life stressing commitment to the quest for excellence, a bond between maker and user, and the belief that good tools contribute to good work.

There was nothing scientific in the process of selecting craftspeople to be represented in this book. Had there been, it wouldn't be authentically western. Virtually everyone interviewed had a different opinion regarding who makes the best saddles, bits and spurs. Answers often varied depending on the respondent's geographic location, age and type of cowboying. Legendary saddle maker Don King, revered for mentoring many of the current master saddlers, believes that such efforts are fruitless. He contends that nobody is the best. Some makers, however, are better for certain types of work or horses. Often, it is more a case of who is better known rather than who is necessarily better. In the course of interviewing all manner of working cowboys, some names cropped up repeatedly. From these, the final cut was made with an eye toward including a mix of established and emerging artisans, regional diversity, different styles and specialty gear. For each artisan in the book, an equally strong case can be made for someone who isn't.

I also make a plea regarding use of the masculine form throughout the book. It is not intended as a slight. Real cowgirls don't need the artificial convention of gender-neutral language to know they are full and equal partners in the western way of life. Many leading artisans are women, such as Montana saddle maker Nancy Petersen. Husband and wife teams, including bit and spur makers Ernie and Teresa Marsh of John Day, Oregon, or Barbara and Jerry Kauffman of Longmont, Colorado, share the joys and trials of the special life they have chosen. In all cases, the steadfast support of a loyal spouse and family is an essential ingredient in the success of these extraordinary artisans.

This book focuses on these artisans and their work. Innovative within the bounds of tradition, beautifully designed and expertly made, their gear rivals or beats that of the old masters. They validate T. S. Eliot's observation, "Each artist who wants to be genuinely innovative must acquire a historic sense." Just as their predecessors developed the traditional techniques and styles mastered by today's gear makers, contemporary craftsmen are adapting new tools, techniques and styles to create tomorrow's traditions. Despite technological innovations, these crafts retain their integrity as artistic expressions of individuals whose unique cultural traditions, identity and values are as viable on the brink of the twenty-first century as when the cowboy emerged on the plains of Texas and California's Pacific Slope 130 years ago. True to the breed, exceptional, gifted artisans continue to forge the tools of the cowboy's trade.

A Cowboy's History of Saddles

Saddle shops are cowboy social clubs where initiated members of the fraternity gather to swap gossip, jokes, horses, tack and saddles. Awash in their camaraderie, the saddle maker goes about his tasks under the watchful eyes of self-appointed experts ready to advise him at all points in the process. A cowboy without an opinion on what constitutes the ideal saddle is about as rare as a cowboy with money in his pocket and a 401K plan.

While each saddle shop is different, they are all the same. Their aroma is universal, evocative as freshly baked bread or newly mown hay. If you grew up in the cowboy West, one whiff of the potent blend of oak-tanned leather, oils and dyes tempered with a little stale Prince Albert or Bull Durham will instantly transport you. No one has ever seen a tidy saddle shop. They are a comforting jumble of works in progress, scraps and pieces of leather, tool-strewn workbenches, and ancient, oil-splattered sewing machines. Within these friendly surroundings, makers craft functional sculptures—the classic western stock saddle.

Fundamental to the trade, the stock saddle allows the cowboy to rope and hold wild cattle, ride rank, broncy colts, and spend grueling hours covering rough ground. The saddle becomes a physical extension of the cowboy, joining horse and rider in perfect union like a latter-day centaur.

The saddle has become a symbol of self-definition. Cowboy songs are salted with references to saddles. A verse to "The Old Chisholm Trail" goes: "I'm going to sell my horse, going to sell my saddle, 'Cause I'm tired of punching these longhorn cattle."

"Selling the saddle" took on great significance in cow country. It became a metaphor for a cowboy's dying. In another context, it meant betraying a trust. Most commonly, however, the phrase was applied to a cowboy who gave up the trade. "Selling the saddle" was an act of both figurative and fiscal significance.

The disparity between a cowboy's wages and good custom gear is most obvious when it's time to buy a new saddle. It represents a major expenditure in an occupation where personal satisfactions exceed financial rewards. Top hands approach the purchase as a capital investment in a tool providing long service with minimal maintenance.

When a buckaroo puts down his hard-earned cash, he is buying more than a contraption for staying on a horse. He is purchasing an object of functional beauty endowed with noble ancestry.

Saddles, like many accoutrements of the cowboys' occupational paraphernalia, have a martial heritage. The western stock saddle descends from the war saddle Spanish conquistadors brought to the New World. Like the proverbial sword beaten to a plowshare, the pacified war saddle made possible the rise of New World

A quintessential saddle shop with works in progress by maker Dusty Harvey. Hamley's, Pendleton, Oregon. (Gear & location courtesy of Loren and Margaret Wood)

A used car lot of saddles. Saddles of all types and vintages await the prospective buyer. (Hamley's. Courtesy of Loren and Margaret Wood)

ranching. It was this basic Mexican saddle that the fledgling American cowboy appropriated and, over time, refined into today's masterpieces.

CALIFORNIO VS. TEXICAN STYLE

All cowboy accoutrements descended from the tradition of the Mexican vaqueros. But in North America, there were two branches of the emergent cowboy family tree, the Texicans and Californios. The Texican progeny spread north, populating the ranges east of the Rockies to Canada's Big Bow River. When they forsook the Lone Star's home range to follow the Polar Star, the Texans rode plain, heavy, square-skirted, double-rigged saddles suited to their hard-and-fast roping style.

From their stomping grounds by the old Pacific's shore, the Californios tribe fanned out to fill the Great Basin country and the ranges of the Northwest. As with the California style of dally roping, these expatriates sat ornate, center-fire, round-skirted saddles appropriated from the native vaqueros.

As these early cowboys filled the western frontier's beckoning voids, they developed regional variants of the two foundation saddle types. Adaptations sprouted from the demands of new working conditions, innovations in construction techniques, the skills and preferences of local saddle makers, and evolving cowboy tastes as to what constituted a stylish rig. The development of unique variations was fostered by the West's vast distances compounded by poor communication and transportation systems.

Variants centered around the major cow towns that sprang up in the wake of the West's expanding ranching empires. As the longhorns trailed north out of Texas, the migration was marked by the rise of Pueblo, and then Denver, Colorado, as important ranching centers. In turn, they were supplanted by Cheyenne, Wyoming, the cowboy Mecca of the plains. In each frontier metropolis, saddlers opened shop to meet the needs of local punchers. In cowboy circles, the towns became synonymous with the saddles made there. Pueblo was associated with the marks of Tom Flynn, Robert Frazier and S. C. Gallup. The "Plains" style saddle, however, reached its zenith at Cheyenne where firms such as Collins and Meanea perfected the double-rigged saddle that traveled north from Texas. Comfortable to man and horse, well suited to all kinds of range work and durable enough to stand up to hard wear and weather, a "Cheyenne rig" was a status symbol in the Great Plains cowboy fraternity.

While their plains brethren were pushing the longhorns toward the northern lights, the Californios went forth, were fruitful, multiplied, and filled the range and basin expanses west of the Great Divide. Saddle makers soon followed the trails blazed in the creation of far-flung cattle empires. Regional makers, including the Visalia Saddle Company of California and Hamley's of Pendleton, Oregon, became favorites with local cowhands. If Cheyenne was the Mecca for the Great Plains waddies, Elko, Nevada, was the holy of holies for the Great Basin buckaroo. In that small Nevada ranching center, firms such as Garcia and Capriola honed the fully stamped, center-fire California saddle with its high cantle and slick forks to an art form, leather thrones for the masters of high-desert cattle kingdoms.

Over time, members of the rival cowboy tribes mingled at the fringes of their range. Fraternization led to the adoption of the other's gear, a cross-fertilization leading to hybridized styles. This process created new saddles exhibiting the parent stock's desired features. After decades of this practice, a predominant stock saddle has evolved in western cow country.

Improvements in communications and transportation that reached even the most remote parts of range country sped this synthesis. The printing of saddle company catalogs was key. A Texas brush popper shading up on a July scorcher or a Wyoming waddie riding out a January blizzard by the bunkhouse stove could thumb through a Hamley or Visalia catalog. Not only did they become familiar with the wares of these distant makers, they could actually order the gear.

Today's Style Blending

Contemporary working saddles reflect a blending of types—the Texas saddle's underlying strength and stability combining with the California saddle's rakish lines and ornamentation. Over the years, the double-rig or rim-fire saddle has emerged as the standard of the working cowboy. Its twin cinches provide greater stability when roping, riding in rough, steep country or breaking a rank colt. Vestiges of the California heritage, however, remain evident in the exquisite tooling and carving that marks a fine custom saddle. Additionally, most saddles now have the more rounded skirts traceable to the original California style.

Within a generation, working cowboys have witnessed a renaissance. Standardized mediocrity is being swept away by individual excellence. Like the turn-of-the-century Arts and Crafts movement that arose in response to the impersonalization of industrial age mass production, the resurgence of fine custom-handcrafted saddles expresses the appreciation of individual creativity, natural materials, and craftsmanship.

Like a modern phoenix, today's custom saddle makers have risen from the ashes of pioneer saddlery firms. The fires that brought them forth burn hottest on the sun-seared, high-desert, Great Basin country of Nevada and Oregon and on the windswept high plains of Wyoming and Montana. Buckaroos and waddies working the ranches of these vast, empty lands kept the coals of tradition smoldering until the winds of the cowboy revival fanned them into a bright blaze, lighting up the West. The entire cowboy fraternity owes a debt to these steadfast keepers of the flame.

An encyclopedic knowledge of French Impressionism and detailed understanding of preparing paint pigments is not necessary to enjoy a Renoir. A cursory familiarity of art history and painting techniques, however, enhances the viewer's enjoyment. So it is with saddles. An exposure to saddle making's history and processes provides a better appreciation of the work of contemporary master craftsmen. While much of this subject matter is esoteric, with little interest to the general public, it is the stuff of passion to saddle makers. Consider the saddletree. Two brothers engaged in the trade fell out over the proper way to make a tree. They hold the other's opinion to be heresy. So acute is the schism, they have not spoken for more than two years. Each waits doggedly for the other to acknowledge his error, repent, and return to the fold of true believers.

The Saddletree

From the horse's perspective, the argument is not trivial. A poorly constructed tree will soon "sore up" the animal's back. Not only does the tree dictate how the saddle fits, it is the skull beneath the skin that determines the saddle's appearance. The "swell" or fullness of the fork is saddlery's equivalent to couture's hemline. While hemlines rise and fall, swells expand and contract.

The skull beneath the skin. A rawhide-covered tree receiving its leather covering.

More than mere fashion statements, different trees reflect a direct connection between form and function. A rodeo roper requires a substantial horn to anchor his "string," while moderate swells and a low cantle facilitate a rapid dismount. At the other end of the arena, the saddle bronc rider has dispensed with a horn altogether and employs large, undercut swells and a high, deeply dished cantle to keep him aboard his draw for the required eight seconds. Between these two extremes is the saddle of the workaday cowboy, occasionally practicing elements of both rodeo skills in the routine performance of his trade.

The profusion of trees available to contemporary makers and their genesis is captured in a panoply of evocative names: The Visalia, Pinto, Hamley Form Fitter, Montana, Ellensburg, Association, Quarter-Horse, Homestead, Low Bronc, Wade, and Toots Mansfield Roper are but a few.

The tree's rawhide sheathing is embedded in range lore. It is a paragon. Strong and durable, rawhide stretches and molds when wet yet shrinks and remains "stiff as ax handle" when dry. In some parts of the West, it is known as "Mexican Iron."

The Leather

Leather, however, is the saddlery trade's basic material. There is nothing like it. The tanning process transforms raw cowhides from a perishable to an imperishable state. Quality saddle leathers are "oak" or vegetable tanned. Naturally produced tannic acids chemically alter the hide, preventing putrefaction and decomposition. Dressing infuses oils and greases into the hide, replacing the natural substances removed in the tanning bath. Dressing provides greater tensile strength, flexibility and water resistance. A consistent supply of quality leather with substance, or thickness, is one of the great challenges facing today's saddle makers. Not only is good saddle leather sometimes hard to come by, it is expensive. In 1989, noted Montana saddle maker Chas Weldon observed that heavy, oak-tanned leather represented approximately $800 of the cost of his most basic saddle, which then sold for $1,500.

To a master saddle maker, a good hide is an object of infinite possibility. Like a sculptor evaluating the potential of a block of marble, the saddle maker reads the hide, looking for flaws that might mar his quest for perfection.

With practiced eye, the maker brings his vision to life, cutting this whole cloth into skirts, jockeys, fenders and the myriad parts forming the saddle. Exactingly cut, shaved and shaped, the pieces of the three-dimensional leather jigsaw puzzle are fitted precisely to the complex angles,

A saddle emerging from a blank canvas of leather.

curves and planes of the horn, forks, seat and cantle. Assuring a smooth, seamless fit is essential for a comfortable, long-wearing saddle. A wrinkle or bulge soon produces a sore back or backside. Ridges or poorly welted seams become stress or friction points, shortening the saddle's life while inviting failure at a critical juncture, such as roping a 2,000-pound bull leaping an arena fence.

Collaborative Design

A truly great saddle is distinguished by more than first-quality materials and meticulous attention to detail during construction. A master craftsman endues it with insightful purpose, based on practical knowledge of the saddle's application. In large measure, this explains why virtually all master saddle makers have been working cowboys or spent a great deal of time in their company. Only direct experience can equip someone to comprehend the complex ergonomic dynamics generated by a powerful, 1,200-pound animal running at 35 miles an hour while packing 200 pounds of saddle and rope-twirling cowboy. Unless you have taken the dally and felt the jerk, you can't appreciate the force generated when a fast-running calf or big steer hits the end of the rope. You savvy your clients' needs better if you've ridden from sunup to sundown over rough country in a driving rain.

The intimate collaboration between maker and user, based on shared experience and common purpose, is not only instrumental to building a truly custom saddle, it also fuels innovation and experimentation. The saddle is still a work in progress. New techniques and ideas are constantly undergoing field testing in sales yards, feedlots, showrings, rodeo arenas and ranges across the West. Introduced at the turn of the century, swell forks were standard on most western saddles by the 1920s. More recently, the Blivins Quick Change Stirrup Buckle was an innovation that simplified adjusting the length of stirrup leathers. Today, the Blivins system has achieved near-universal acceptance. Developing a better rigging system is an area where the search for improvement continues. So long as real cowboys ride long and hard and saddle makers pour talent and heart into their work, the quest for the perfect saddle will remain a never-ending saga.

The moment of truth: putting your string on a ton of bull at the Pendleton Round-Up.

The Saddler's Art

A chapter in that story must be devoted to the pursuit of artistic expression. Western stock saddles have always had a decorative dimension—fine stamping and a flash of silver being greatly admired by cowboys. To men living in dirt-floored dugouts or raw-lumbered shacks, it was as close to wallpaper or fancy furniture as they would come. True to the breed, today's cowboys are still partial to a little flash in their rigs.

Each custom saddle is a blank canvas challenging the artisan's muse. Carefully wetted and prepared, the leather becomes a pliable, malleable medium. Pounding and gouging with hammer, blade, stamp and chisel, the maker adorns his kinetic sculpture with bas-relief murals. Definition, depth, balance and symmetry are

The skilled hands of a master artisan transform blank leather into an object of beauty.

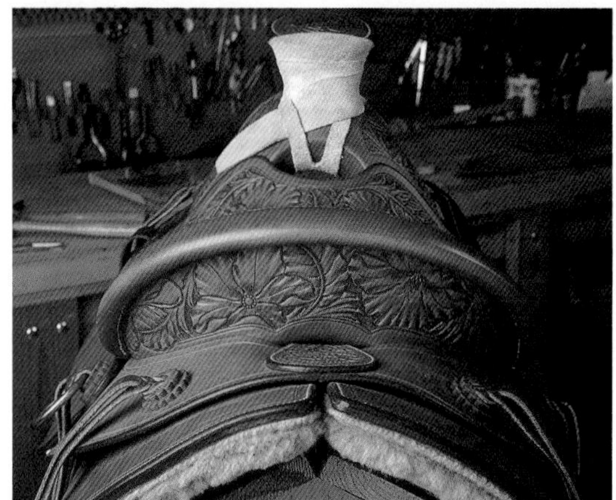

Chuck Stormes' floral decorative tooling. (Saddle courtesy of D. D. Potter)

hallmarks of fine tooling. Master artisans "paint" the leather with hard-edged tools, creating visual drama through depth, pattern, texture, line and shadow. Burnishing, staining, oiling and varnishing the leather creates a finish of rich, subtle luster. The artisan employs the patina to complement the saddle's underlying tooling patterns just as a sculptor uses different finishes to bring greater character to his castings.

Resonating with echoes of the Alhambra, traditional stamping patterns reflect their Spanish and Moorish heritage. Like the Alhambra's gardens, a saddle's botanical motif brings an earthly delight to hot and dusty lands. The Oak Leaf and Wild Rose are the foundation patterns of floral decorative tooling. Executed with subtle variation, they are employed by virtually all saddle makers. A third standard pattern is the Basket Weave, providing a counterpoint to the Oak Leaf and Wild Rose's floral profusion. Its geometric precision represents man's quest to bring order to nature's verdant free forms. These patterns provide a basis for comparison between makers. Executed by a master leather worker such as Don King of Sheridan, Wyoming, the Wild Rose is as distinctive a signature as Charlie Russell's buffalo skull. They also form the foundation for building innovative new designs. When Hermiston, Oregon, saddle maker Rich Boyer saw a mulberry leaf floating down an irrigation ditch in his pasture, he was captivated by its potential as a stamping pattern. His years of practice with traditional designs enabled him to translate the mulberry leaf from nature to leather.

Carving and tooling are not the only avenues of creative embellishment available to the artisan. Touches that include decorative stitching, lacing, and rawhide cantle and horn counters add understated flair. Even saddle strings and conchos provide additional scope for expression. The flash of silver, however, is the most dramatic fillip. Tastefully restrained, it can be found on working saddles, marrying the fruit of the silversmith and saddler's labors in complementary harmony.

The Spirit of Contemporary Saddle Making

While saddle making is a traditional craft employing traditional techniques, it is distinguished by the evident freshness and vitality among contemporary practitioners. In an increasingly jaded world given to the bland and banal, the work of today's master saddlers retains its integrity and originality. Like members of the earlier Arts and Crafts movement, today's top contemporary saddle makers are passionately committed to their trade and its associated way of life. Often, you gain a better insight into someone's character through their hobbies rather than their work. With saddlers, what they do is integral to who they are. They pour themselves into their creations, with skilled hands infusing their spirit into the functional art they produce.

Their passion is not to slavishly reproduce the old masters' work. Rather, within the bounds of functional requirements they pursue a saddle that is more comfortable, longer lasting and stronger than any ever made. When a maker creates a custom saddle, it is for a specific customer. Frequently, the client is a friend or highly regarded hand who has come to them seeking the best. While the saddler strives to make a saddle to win the praise of that demanding customer, a great craftsman is his own harshest critic. If he is not satisfied with a seam or the alignment of a component part that would be covered up deep within the saddle's interior, out of sight to all but the maker, the great saddler will undo several hours of work to make the hidden flaw perfect. To survive and flourish, the working saddle has to be genuine, solid and true to its core.

When a real cowboy's saddle goes out the shop door, it is facing a life of hard use and abuse. Their saddles are created to face the trial by ordeal of honest, rough, ranch and rodeo work. They will live in a world of sweat and strain, downpour and drought, seldom knowing the soothing touch of saddle soap and leather balm. It is a setting where only the best will survive the test of time. It is a challenge that a crop of exceptional craftsmen has accepted.

Today, there are more talented, dedicated saddle makers plying their craft from the mesquite thickets of Texas to Alberta's windswept plains to the grassy hillsides of California's Pacific Slope than at any time in history. They have refined the craft they inherited and taken it to a level undreamed of by the masters of the long-ago, open-range days.

The saddle makers featured in this book are representative of this renaissance, standing for all their proud guild's members. Each works at the very top of his or her profession and shares the ultimate accolade of recommendation by real working cowboys who prize their masterworks.

They also serve who stand and wait. Many top hands own several saddles, a major investment.

SADDLE MAKERS

DALE HARWOOD

Dale Harwood is the saddle maker's saddle maker. Respected by fellow craftsmen and top horsemen, his saddles set the standard for measuring quality workmanship. Many knowledgeable students of the trade consider him the greatest living saddle maker. When asking saddle makers whose kack they would ride if not their own, the name most frequently mentioned is Dale Harwood. Harwood's true legacy will be more than saddles bearing his mark. It will also be Dale's profound influence on the trade and mentorship of a generation of aspiring saddle makers. Imparting more than technique, his example conveys pride in the trade, absolute integrity and an abiding quest for perfection.

To working cowboys, Harwood saddles are treasured possessions; they willingly wait years to own one of his masterpieces. The boss of a large eastern Oregon ranch typifies proud ownership of Harwood saddles. His house is unlocked, the car and pickup are parked with keys in the ignition, and the barn door stands open. His Harwood saddles, however, are securely stored under lock and key.

Making saddles is all Harwood has ever wanted to do. Getting a start, however, was not easy. When he approached saddle makers with his interest, cold shoulders were the usual response. Dale quickly learned that the best

Rich luster and fine carving distinguish Dale Harwood's work. (Saddle courtesy of the Roberts family)

strategy for gathering information was to engage the craftsman in conversation on an unrelated topic and gradually work the discussion around to saddle making. While becoming an authority on fishing and politics, Harwood also learned a little about saddle making. Despite the closed-shop mentality of his formative years, Dale did find help among established artisans that included Ray Holes and Dale Knight. Even so, he learned saddle making primarily in the school of hard knocks through trial and error.

Harwood is a leading scholar of the trade. Exhaustively researching the profession, he has amassed an extensive library of saddle-making materials. Having devoted his career to rediscovering the trade's lost secrets, Dale is dedicated to passing them on to tomorrow's saddlers. Renowned for sharing information and tips with makers serious about the trade, he often spends hours helping them at the expense of his own business. Harwood's philosophy is, "If you want help, go to the best person you can find in the field. People who are reluctant to share information are often hiding their own lack of knowledge." Thanks in part to Harwood's attitude, a remarkable spirit of cooperation, rather than professional jealousy, permeates the top levels of saddle making.

No matter how good a saddler is, he is at the mercy of the saddletree maker. Opting to control his destiny, Harwood makes his trees, dictating absolute quality from start to finish. This control extends to processing his own rawhide.

Reminiscing on his thirty-four years in the trade, Harwood observed that making western gear is a cyclical boom-and-bust business tied to cattle prices. When cattle are up, saddle sales rise. When they take a drop, orders follow them down. A process of natural selection, it eliminates the fringe makers, leaving only the dedicated and talented ones. Harwood qualifies on both counts.

Under Harwood's benevolent stewardship, quality saddlery has gone from the brink of a lost art to the verge of a new golden age. That age will include Harwood's sons, who work alongside him in the family business, a source of satisfaction to a proud father. A dynasty in the making, Harwoods will carry the craft into the next century and to new heights.

A classic Dale Harwood saddle. (Saddle courtesy of the Roberts family)

EDDIE BROOKS

Eddie Brooks is a transcendent figure in contemporary saddle making, bridging the gap between the Texas and California schools. It is an accomplishment almost as difficult as bringing peace to the Balkans or Middle East. How a Texas-born, raised and trained maker became the dean of buckaroo saddlery is a story worth telling.

Eddie grew up cowboying and rodeoing in the Texas tradition. A bareback and bull rider, his love of the sport drew him down the West's long, lonely roads. Outside the rodeo arena, Eddie pursued another love, leather working.

Brooks learned the trade with the celebrated Leddy brothers, making classic Texas-style saddles. Their custom-order shop afforded him the opportunity to master all aspects of the craft. Eddie's talent caught the attention of Paul Bear, owner of the venerable buckaroo firm Capriola's in Elko, Nevada. Bear hired Brooks to infuse new ideas and techniques into the traditional Nevada slick-fork, single-rig saddles. Brooks arrived at Bear's ranch just as a phone call informed Bear his cattle were on the railroad tracks. Pressed into buckaroo service, Eddie helped round them up on a horse fitted with a spade bit and wood-horned, slick-forked saddle. To his amazement, the other riders set out posting the trot, a sacrilege in Texas. A hard and fast roper, he was astounded watching the local hands swing big loops and take their dallies. Eddie wondered just what kind of a deal he was getting into, but he decided to sign on.

Mastering the California style made Brooks a better saddle maker. He was forced to bear down and concentrate on basics. Nevada buckaroos covered vast, open ranges. Riding all day demanded a saddle that fit both horse and rider. Many knowledgeable horsemen claim Eddie Brooks puts a better seat in the saddle than anyone. One described the sensation as "sitting in the saddle rather than on it." Putting it more colorfully, an Elko cowboy says the seat in a Brooks saddle "makes your butt giggle."

Nevada saddle making also opened new vistas for carving, tooling and silver ornamentation. Makers at Capriola's were encouraged to refine their artistic talents and pioneer new patterns and styles. The whole saddle was a canvas. Eddie created harmonized design compositions, complementing the saddle's underlying form. Beautifully conceived and executed, Eddie's saddles are high art.

After several years as foreman of Capriola's saddle shop, Brooks went into business for himself. Soon he had developed a loyal and appreciative following. Eddie admits that while he wouldn't turn down more money, he's not interested in fancy things. So long as he has "beans on the table and the respect of top hands," Brooks is satisfied.

Formerly, makers priced saddles with a formula of one-third materials, one-third labor and one-third profit. Now Brooks is happy to recover his labor and material costs before worrying over profits. Putting the dilemma in perspective, Eddie remembers when a good tree cost less than $20, top-quality leather went for $.25 a pound, and base-priced Capriola saddles cost $225. Today, a custom tree costs more than $300, while top-grade saddle leather goes for $8 a pound.

Building saddles to meet changing conditions tests the maker's ability. Even tradition-revering Nevada buckaroos have changed the way they cowboy. When Eddie first moved to Elko, many Nevada horses weren't broke to the back cinch. Today, horses are bigger and stronger with higher withers. Accordingly, trees have been modified with the front rigging moved further ahead, rear cinches are now standard and seats must be adjusted accordingly. Eddie says that change forces him to focus on basics and continually improve his skills. After years at the top of the profession, and with three years' worth of orders on the books, each saddle remains a fresh challenge with lessons to learn.

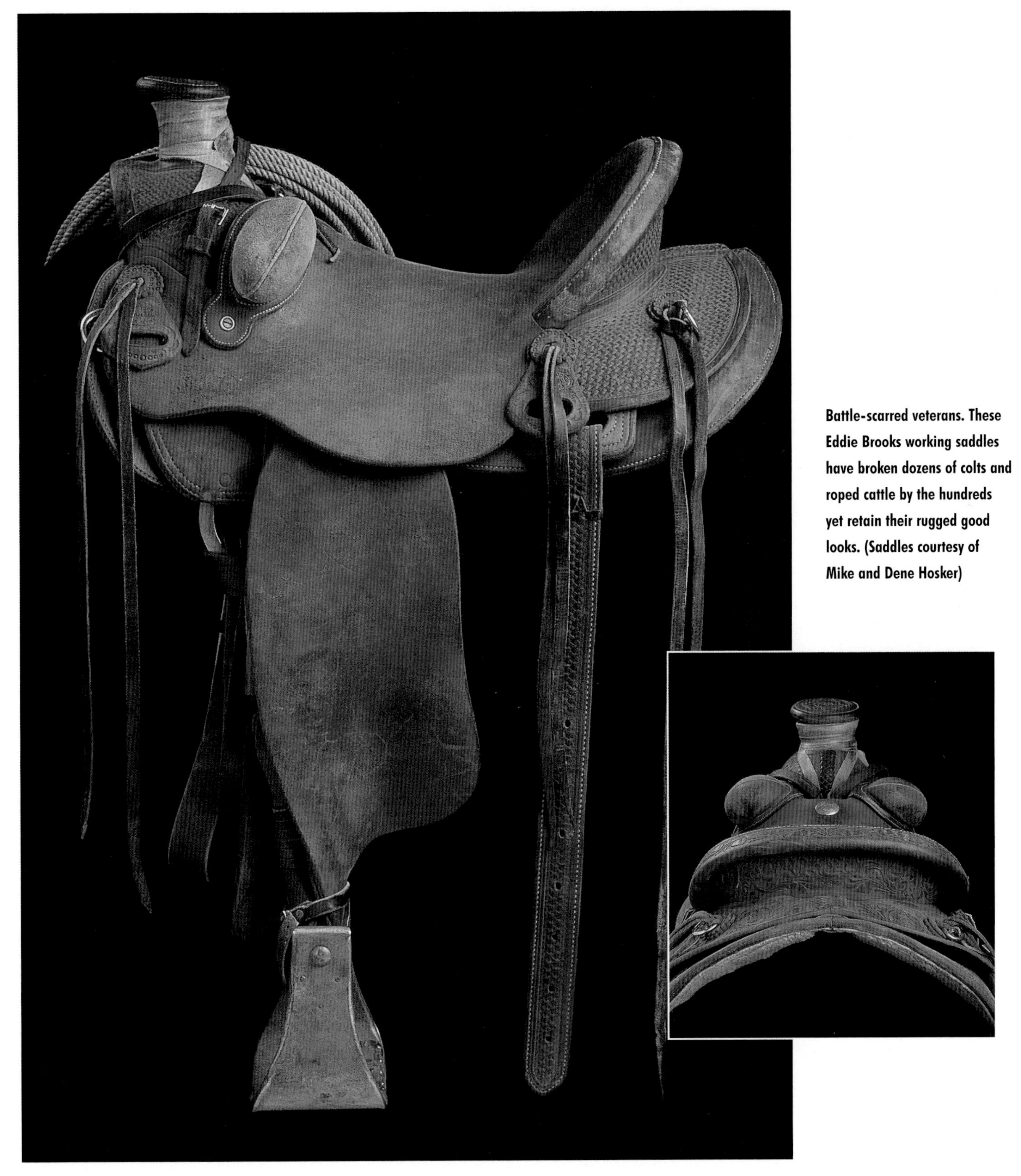

Battle-scarred veterans. These Eddie Brooks working saddles have broken dozens of colts and roped cattle by the hundreds yet retain their rugged good looks. (Saddles courtesy of Mike and Dene Hosker)

A Rich Boyer saddle awaits delivery to another satisfied customer.

Rich Boyer

From his shop incongruously perched on a balcony overlooking Roemark's, the finest clothing store in Hermiston, Oregon, Rich Boyer turns out some of the most sought-after saddles in the Pacific Northwest. Boyer's saddles haven't yet been discovered by collectors; they are real using rigs. His clientele is made up of salt-of-the-earth working cowboys. They ride the muddy, mundane pens and alleyways of feedlots, break colts, scrape out a living selling horses through the auction ring, train cutting and reining horses, ranch the high deserts and mountain valleys of the Columbia Basin or ply their trade in the rodeo arena.

A Rich Boyer saddle is a prized possession in their lives. A chance encounter on an eastern Oregon back road made this abundantly clear in classic western fashion—a conversation leaning against the side of a pickup, parked haphazardly along the roadside. When asked what he thought of his new Boyer saddle, the owner reached into the cab, flipped down the sun visor, pulled out a photo of the saddle and showed it with the happy pride of a new parent.

For Rich, earning his living exclusively by making saddles is a dream realized. Originally a working cowboy, he rode for ranches in central Oregon. Out of financial necessity, he often repaired his own saddles. He began studying saddle construction. This investigation led to discussions with a local saddle maker, Sandy Anderson of Burns, Oregon. Their friendship, and Rich's interest, grew. When Anderson decided to retire, he offered to sell the shop to Rich and help him learn the trade. Shortly after consummating the deal, Sandy died suddenly.

With little training, Rich found himself in the leather-working business. The path from neophyte to master craftsman was largely one of experimentation and self-discovery.

In the early days, the shop was in the back of Rich's house. He survived primarily on repair work supplemented by riding for local ranches while he built his first saddles. His goal was a good-fitting, comfortable and strong using rather than showy saddle. Rich's years on the hurricane deck were invaluable, providing insight into what is important in a using saddle. Strength and durability remain hallmarks of his kacks. Like an automobile manufacturer road testing a car, Boyer often has National Finals Rodeo (NFR) pickup man Pat Beard try out his saddles to ensure they are stout. Rich figures there is no greater test of a saddle than tying onto two thousand pounds of enraged bull and dragging it out of the arena.

Seeking greater financial stability, he signed on as the saddle maker for the legendary Hamley Company of Pendleton, Oregon. In his years

Finish work of a Boyer saddle.

with the venerable firm, he refined his carving and stamping skills, making trophy saddles for the world-famous Pendleton Round-Up. Answering the siren call of having his own shop again, he hung up his shingle in Hermiston, Oregon. While Hermiston lacks the rich history and romance of more famous western towns, it is a hotbed of cowboy activity.

In recent years, Rich's concern with the saddle's appearance has grown to match his passion for fit and strength. His original mulberry pattern has become a signature. Making trophy saddles, such as those for the Pendleton Round-Up and Hermiston's Farm City Pro Rodeo, gives him the opportunity to indulge in elaborate, intricate carving and stamping, which the average cowboy can't afford.

Notable patrons of Rich's shop include top timed-event hands such as the Currin brothers—Tony, Steve and Ron—who have qualified

Road testing. NFR Pickup Man Pat Beard puts a Boyer saddle through its paces.

for the NFR. Collectively, they have won over sixty trophy saddles, many by leading custom makers, yet they choose to ride rigs made by Rich to cover the rugged, sprawling terrain of their family ranch. The most noted user, and perhaps most ardent spokesman, for Rich's saddles is many-time World Champion Calf Roper Joe Beaver. Joe has his choice of any saddle in the world to ride. He chooses Rich Boyer's.

NANCY PETERSEN

Affirming Will Rogers' observation that "Women are not the weak, frail, little flowers that they are advertised. There has never been anything invented yet, including war, that a man would enter into, that a woman wouldn't, too," women are entering the male province of saddle making. Artisans such as Nancy Petersen are building quality saddles with the fresh, unique perspective of the feminine persuasion.

Nancy Petersen is a leading maker, praised for her exceptional saddles. She is respected as a great saddle maker, not a great woman saddle maker. Nancy's saddles are prized by working ranch people—men and women—who appreciate quality gear. Striking and well spoken, Nancy is more likely to be taken for a successful lawyer or business executive than a top saddle maker. For Petersen, the decision to take up the trade was not an expression of feminism but rather a business reality. She and her husband, Carl, run a western store and saddle shop in Three Forks, Montana. While Nancy did some general saddle repairs and leather work, the shop always employed a saddle maker. In a lament shared by many, they found constant challenge in keeping a good saddle maker in the store. Talented makers either set up shop for themselves or were of the tumbleweed breed who just have to move on every few years.

Faced with constant turnover, the Petersens decided their solution lay in Nancy's becoming a full-fledged saddle maker. With leather-working and saddle-repair experience, she had a leg up on the process. Combined with native ability and dedication, she was well on the way to becoming a good saddle maker. Mentorship from an exceptional group of saddle makers made her an accomplished craftswoman. Nancy's mentors are the saddlery equivalent of an Ivy League faculty. Among them is the renowned Don King. Both Jim Lathrup—considered by some experts to be one of the ten best saddle makers in the world—and rising talent Mark Broger worked for the Petersens. Nancy especially credits Bob Kelly, an alumnus of the famous Ray Holes Saddlery, with helping her learn the trade.

Being a woman in a traditionally male-oriented trade has proven as much a help as a hindrance. While there may be a few backcountry mossy backs who wouldn't ride a saddle made by a woman, women have been good customers. Nancy builds saddles for them reflecting a woman's unique perspective. Her ladies' saddles are more than lighter-weight versions of men's rigs. The female pelvic structure causes women

A hard-working beauty. This Nancy Petersen saddle is used every day on the range and in the rodeo arena. (Saddle courtesy of Jane Glennie-Carlson)

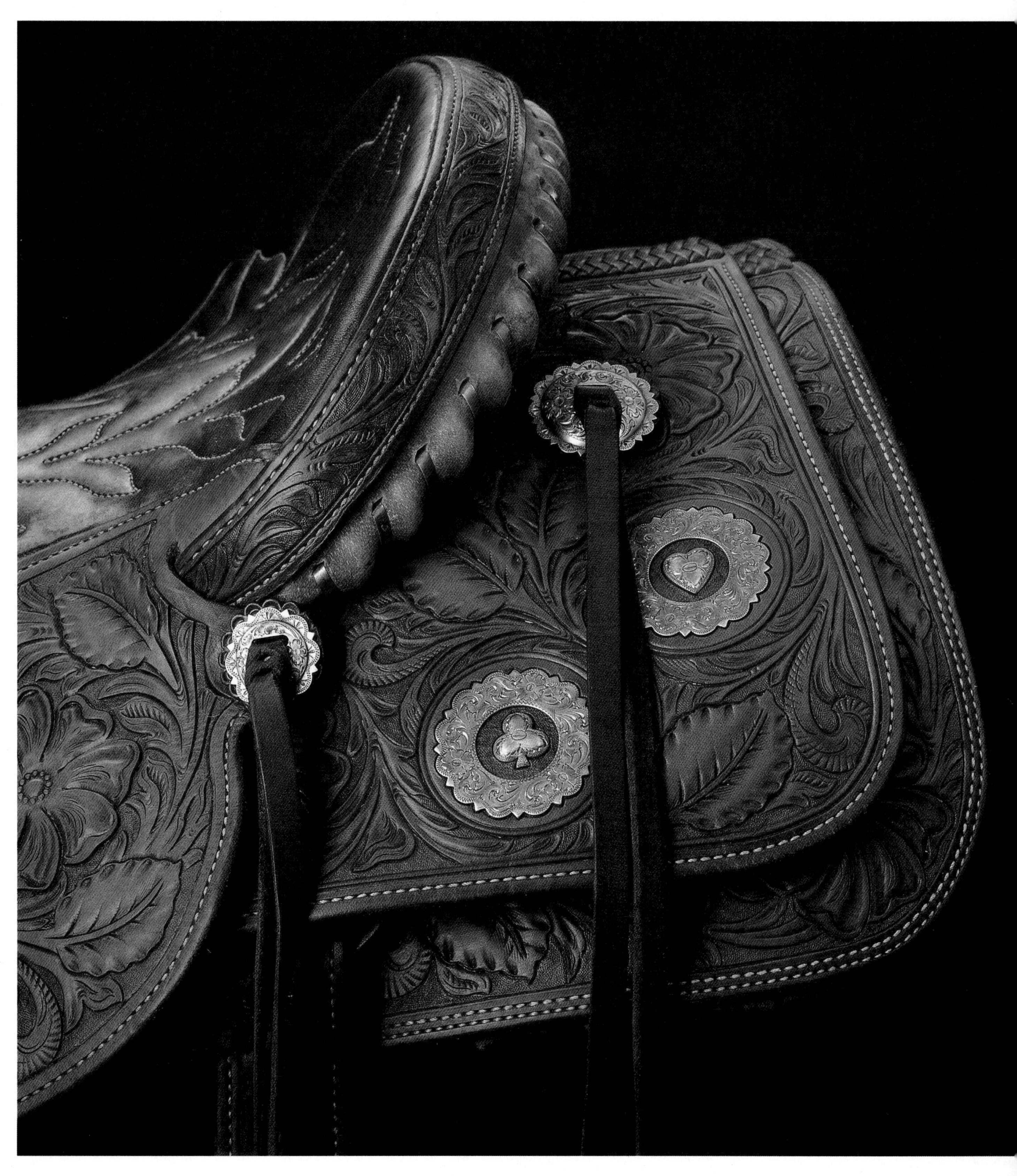

A winning combination, Petersen's fine tooling and Bob Schaezlein's silverwork transform the saddle into an object of functional beauty. (Saddle courtesy of Jane Glennie-Carlson)

to sit a horse differently. In building a "ground," or underlying seat, to accommodate this anatomical variance, Petersen customizes her saddles for women. Nancy is able to personalize the seat, matching the customer's riding style. More aggressive riders, particularly those with an English-style background, prefer a forward seat. Others are more comfortable and secure with a deeper center seat.

Nancy does not, however, consider herself a "women's" saddle maker. More saddles for men than women have left her shop. Her goal is building high-quality using rigs that meet the desires of the customer rather than associating with any specific tree or type of saddle. Of particular concern is putting a good seat in the saddle. Her own experience as an accomplished horsewoman is a great help in this quest. In addition to general ranch work, Nancy competes in roping and barrel-racing events on the Montana rodeo circuit. Consequently, her roping saddles enjoy a large following. That Don King has purchased one of Nancy's saddles for his museum in Sheridan, Wyoming, gives Nancy's work the saddle maker's version of the Good Housekeeping seal of approval.

Beyond the basics of building a finely crafted tool, Nancy enjoys the challenge of decorative carving and stamping. She describes her stamping style as a mix between the King-inspired Sheridan style, Ray Holes' work, and the Severe brothers' look. Each year, Petersen tries to make a few trophy saddles. These projects provide considerable artistic license for elaborate tooling and carving, which many of her working ranch clients cannot afford. Nancy has special reason to lavish her talents on trophy saddles, for there is a good chance they will remain at home. Her daughter, a top circuit competitor, won one of Nancy's trophy saddles—the ultimate in "keeping it in the family."

Nancy loves her trade without being a slave to it. She is active in the community and a fixture in Montana rodeo circles as well as being devoted to her family. Like other, more conventional, career women, she has found the elusive key to balancing work, family and her own interests—no small feat in itself. Nancy Petersen enjoys the western woman's version of having it all.

Weathering the storm. A Severe bronc saddle in action.

The Severe Brothers

Pendleton, Oregon, is a town of institutions: the Round-Up, Happy Canyon, the Let 'Er Buck Room, the woolen mills with its Indian blankets, Hamley's, and the Severe Brothers Saddle Shop. While most saddle makers—even those famous within the trade—toil in relative obscurity, the Severes have achieved widespread recognition. Featured in advertisements for Wrangler jeans and Blitz-Weinhardt breweries, captured in bronze and paint by leading western artists and honored by the Smithsonian Institution, Duff Severe may be the world's most recognized saddle maker. He oversees a multigenerational family enterprise producing some of the world's best saddles.

The founders, Duff, and his late brother Bill, were raised in Idaho ranch country. Lifelong craftsmen, they grew up as rawhiders, a skill practiced by their father. The firm's motto, "Rawhide Quality," acknowledges their beginnings. After World War II, Hamley's was offering G.I. Bill apprenticeships. Freshly minted civilians, the brothers signed on to learn the saddlery trade. With the luck of the draw, Bill ended up in the tree shop while Duff was assigned to learn leather working.

They learned from some of the best in the business. Drawing on their training, Duff and Bill made the first saddle bearing the famous Severe sunburst mark in 1954. The brothers launched their shop in 1955, and as the story line goes, the rest is history.

Fit for a champion. Butch Knowles' Pendleton Round-Up trophy bronc saddle made by the Severe Brothers.

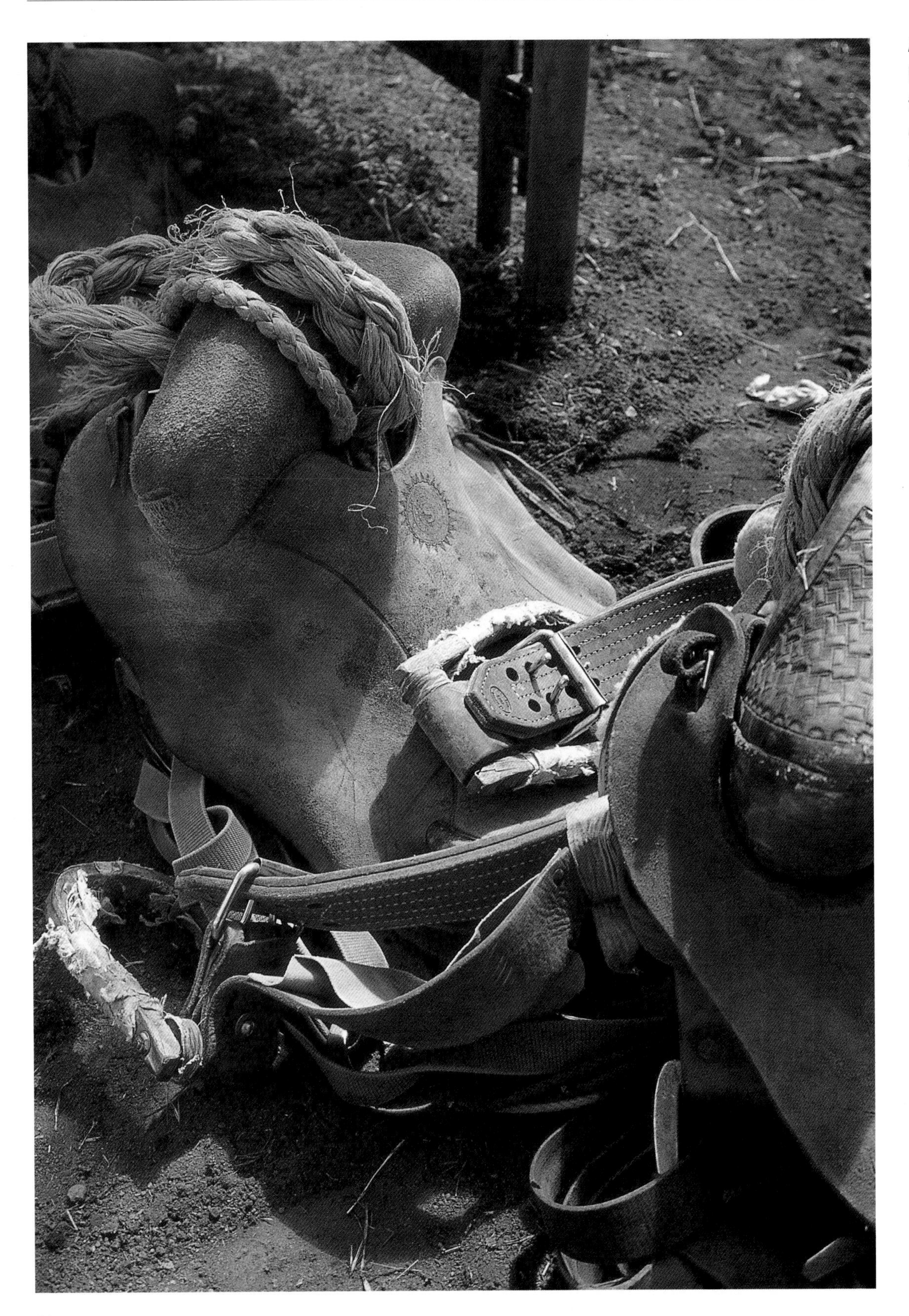

A day's work done. Severe bronc saddles with their famous sunburst trademark await their owners at the stripping chute.

Born in Pendleton, the "Association" bronc saddle is a classic tool of the trade. From the beginning, the name Severe and bronc saddles were synonymous. The Severe bronc saddle is the standard of the industry, prized by the world's greatest riders. Rodeo legends Casey Tibbs, Larry Mahan, Bill Smith and Clint Johnson rode Severes to world championships. Building rigs tough enough to stand up to the punishment inflicted by a chute-fighting bronc may be saddlery's ultimate test. It is a challenge the Severes relish. Their prior rawhiding experience was invaluable, allowing them to select and process the tree's rawhide covering. Duff maintains that thick, perfectly prepared bullhide is the secret to their bronc saddle's phenomenal strength. Former champion bronc rider Doug Brown still uses a saddle Duff made the year they opened shop, proof positive of enduring toughness.

If you can build bronc saddles that survive the thrashing of the world's best bucking stock, your stock saddles will take ranch life's routine travails in stride. Severe stock saddles rapidly attracted a large and devoted following among working cowboys. Bill and Duff consulted with the region's top hands, incorporating their observations and preferences. Able to build saddles from start to finish in-house, they created rigs of exceptional quality. They pioneered a unique Severe style, featuring scroll-cut carving and decorative rawhide work.

Over the years, the shop became a cowboy social center. In a tradition dating to the firm's fledgling days, the Severes opened the bunkhouse adjacent to the saddle shop to Round-Up contestants needing a place to stay. The "Hotel de Round-Up"'s registries, a series of leather scrolls, are a log of rodeo history.

When Bill's sons, Robin, Monte and Randy, grew old enough, they began learning the trade. Uncle Duff summarized saddle making to them as "a medieval product built with medieval tools for medieval wages." His philosophy was, "The cow gave its all for the saddle, the least you can give is your best."

In 1982, the Smithsonian Institution inducted Duff as a Master Traditional Artist, the first leather craftsman so honored. The Severes are frequently invited to display their work at the Smithsonian and participate in festivals celebrating the nation's master craftspeople. The Western and English Equipment Manufacturers Association has also awarded Duff its Lifetime Achievement Award. The recognition that matters most, however, is that of top rodeo and working cowboys.

While Randy and his brothers enjoy being part of a tradition, they are not content to rest on the family's laurels. The current generation continues to improve and refine its saddles, making subtle changes in response to improvements in equine conformation and performance. Today, when a horse leaves the roping box, "it's like riding a rocket." Consequently, general cowboying and specialty competition saddles have been modified with higher cantles and shorter seats. At the other end of the arena, bronc twisters now "ride the front end," preferring a longer seat to keep the cantle out of the way.

To solve the backlog problem plaguing most leading saddle makers the Severes have adopted a novel solution. In January, they start taking orders, first come, first served. When they have a year's worth of work, the books are closed. The order book reveals the extent and diversity of their clientele, including recording star Chris LeDoux, Hollywood legend Clint Eastwood and former President Gerald Ford. An incident at a small rodeo, however, captured the essence of what Severe saddles mean to working cowboys. A young nephew of rodeo champion Bill Smith won a check in the bronc riding. Asked his plans for the money, the cowboy replied without hesitation, "I'm going to make a deposit on a Severe saddle of my own. By the time it's ready, I'll have earned enough to pay for it."

Champion cowboy Tony Currin's Chester Hape trophy saddle.

CHESTER HAPE

In Sheridan, Wyoming, you can't throw your hat without hitting a world-class saddle maker. Sheridan's saddlery fraternity includes the likes of Don King, perhaps the West's most acclaimed saddler, his talented son John, Billy Gardner, Don Butler and Chester Hape. Of this illustrious group, Hape might be the greatest leather worker, raising saddle making to a high art form. The Big Horn Gallery in Cody, Wyoming, exhibits his work alongside that of leading western painters and sculptors.

Although he was ranch raised and has been around rodeo and show arenas most of his life, Hape's far-flung interests differentiate him from many of his contemporaries. An avid windsurfer, he shares the sport's exhilaration with enthusiasts half his age. His other hobbies are running marathons and competing in Iron Man triathlons.

These intensely physical activities contrast starkly to the sedentary saddlery trade. For Hape, the contrast must be cathartic, for he is able to approach leather working with total concentration. His specialty is very fancy, elaborately tooled and decorated saddles. Hape's trophy saddles, made for the Professional Rodeo Cowboy Association (PRCA), grace the Cowboy Hall of Fame and the homes of rodeo's greatest champions. While he established his reputation in trophy saddles, Chester now applies his master's touch to all types: show, buckaroo, roping and reproductions of earlier styles. He particularly enjoys making buckaroo-type saddles because they are more practical than show saddles yet still have "a lot of flash." No matter how fancy the saddle, Chester prides himself that "a cowboy can put it on his horse and use it."

For Hape, the luxury of being able to pick the projects he wants to do while exploring the saddle's artistic potential has increased his enjoyment of the trade. His current artistic freedom

has been hard earned, the product of thirty-five diligent years of toiling at the trade. As a youngster, he was tutored by two exceptional leather workers, Rudy Mudra and Lloyd Davis. Together, they helped found the Sheridan "school." Later, he worked for the Otto F. Ernst Saddlery, where he met Don King, the man who had the greatest influence on his career.

For Hape, the western revival movement with its Trappings-type shows emphasizing artistry has been a boon to his career. If the stock saddle is indeed an art form, students will study Chester Hape's work like young painters in the Louvre copy the great masters—not for copying's sake but to learn the brush strokes, composition and use of color that equals genius. Hape frequently sees his influence in other makers' trophy saddles. Young saddle maker Monte Beckman, known for his use of nontraditional stamping patterns, cites Hape's work as that which he most admires.

The most eloquent tribute to Hape's artistry is a lone picture pinned above the workbench of saddler Randy Severe. It's a photograph of a saddle Chester made for a raffle at the NFR. Randy keeps it there as an inspiration. To him, "It's the most beautiful saddle I've ever seen."

Exquisite tooling has earned Chester Hape acclaim as a master leather worker. (Saddle courtesy of Tony and Kelli Currin)

MONTE BECKMAN

Monte Beckman is heir to the rolling-stone tradition of early saddle makers who moved from one cow town to another. South Dakota born, Oregon raised and trained as a saddle maker in Washington, he has plied the trade in California, New Mexico, Oregon and Utah. His odyssey began on the family ranch in South Dakota where he received an early exposure to leather working. Monte's uncles were noted leather toolers and carvers.

As a teenager, Beckman moved with his family to the cow country around Burns, Oregon. Following the buckaroo country's traditional rite of passage, he cowboyed while going to school and had a fling at rodeoing after graduation. He quickly realized that being "a human lawn dart" was no fun and his primary contribution to the sport of bronc riding was sweetening the pot for the other contestants.

Monte's withdrawal from the rodeo arena coincided with his plunge into the waters of matrimony. By happenstance, the newlyweds' landlord was also a saddler. Beckman often found himself hanging around his postage-stamp-sized shop, "bugging him with questions about saddle making."

Before he could pursue his budding interest, Monte had a four-year hiatus from cowboying and saddle making thanks to Uncle Sam. Returning to civilian life, he set up a welding and machine shop and shod horses. While the business provided a decent living, Beckman didn't

Monte Beckman's gun-engraving-inspired leather tooling. (Saddle courtesy of Loren and Margaret Wood)

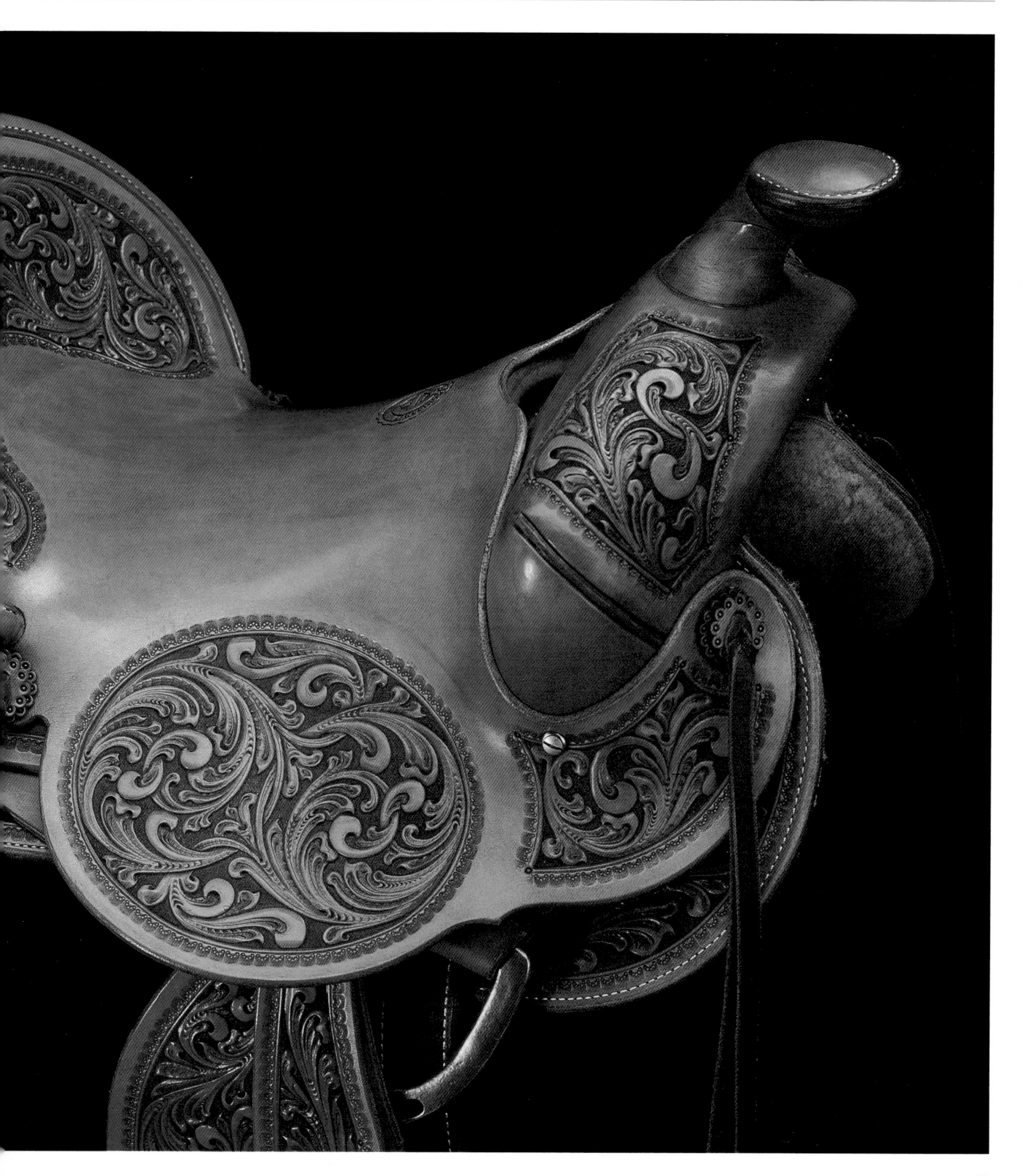

find the work rewarding. Remembering his earlier interest in saddle making, he set out to find someone to teach him the trade, a task that proved almost as challenging as the craft itself. Eventually, he convinced a Spokane, Washington, saddle maker, Bill Long, to take him on. From the beginning, Beckman knew he had found his calling. In addition to the mentorship of Long, Monte also credits Duff Severe and Carl Elmer with influencing his development.

After an all-too-short apprenticeship, Monte found himself facing the harsh realities of trying to earn a living making saddles. Over the years he plied the trade in a variety of places, either on his own or working for saddle shops. Throughout his journeys, however, Beckman kept his vision focused on mastering the craft, always seeking to improve his skills. Beckman believes a quality saddle begins with, "paying attention to detail from step one." Solid and comfortable, a Beckman saddle is practical as well as pretty.

This is borne out by the number of working cowboys who order his rigs. Having done it himself, Monte feels a special affinity for men and women who earn their living on horseback. Rapport with the customer is critical to Monte's approach to saddle making because he believes the ability to "transfer the customer's vision into leather" is essential.

Creating visions in leather is Monte's stock in trade. He appreciates the work of foundation and contemporary master toolers, particularly that of Chester Hape, but his principle inspiration comes from gun engraving. Unusual and dramatic, his patterns get lots of comments. Monte takes it as a compliment when he sees his designs copied by other makers. Among saddlers, imitation is indeed the sincerest form of flattery. Bit, spur and silver makers are often drawn to Beckman's saddles. So much so that some have proposed collaborative efforts, matching the bit and spur's engraving to the saddle's tooling.

Often the difference between a well-known and obscure saddle maker is not the quality of their work but how famous their customers are. Monte estimates that half of his orders come from the word-of-mouth reputation of his saddles and the other half is generated by participation in events such as Elko's Cowboy Poetry Gathering, major horse sales and rodeos, including Cowboy Christmas at the NFR. As his business has begun to grow, however, Monte finds that he now spends more time in the shop keeping up with orders than on the road generating them.

Monte's tumbleweed days may be over, for he is putting down roots in Moab, Utah's, exotically beautiful canyon country. His tree maker also lives in the area, and working directly with him "sure solves a whole lot of problems." Since Moab is now a popular destination for European tourists, they have provided Monte with an unlikely source of business.

Happily at rest and beginning to prosper, Monte has no regrets. Reflecting on his career choice, he says, "I love building saddles—but it sure ain't a get-rich-quick scheme." To a man who loves what he is doing, however, it has rewards that can never be tallied in a ledger book.

Monte Beckman's commemorative 75th Anniversary Association Saddle. (Saddle courtesy of Loren and Margaret Wood)

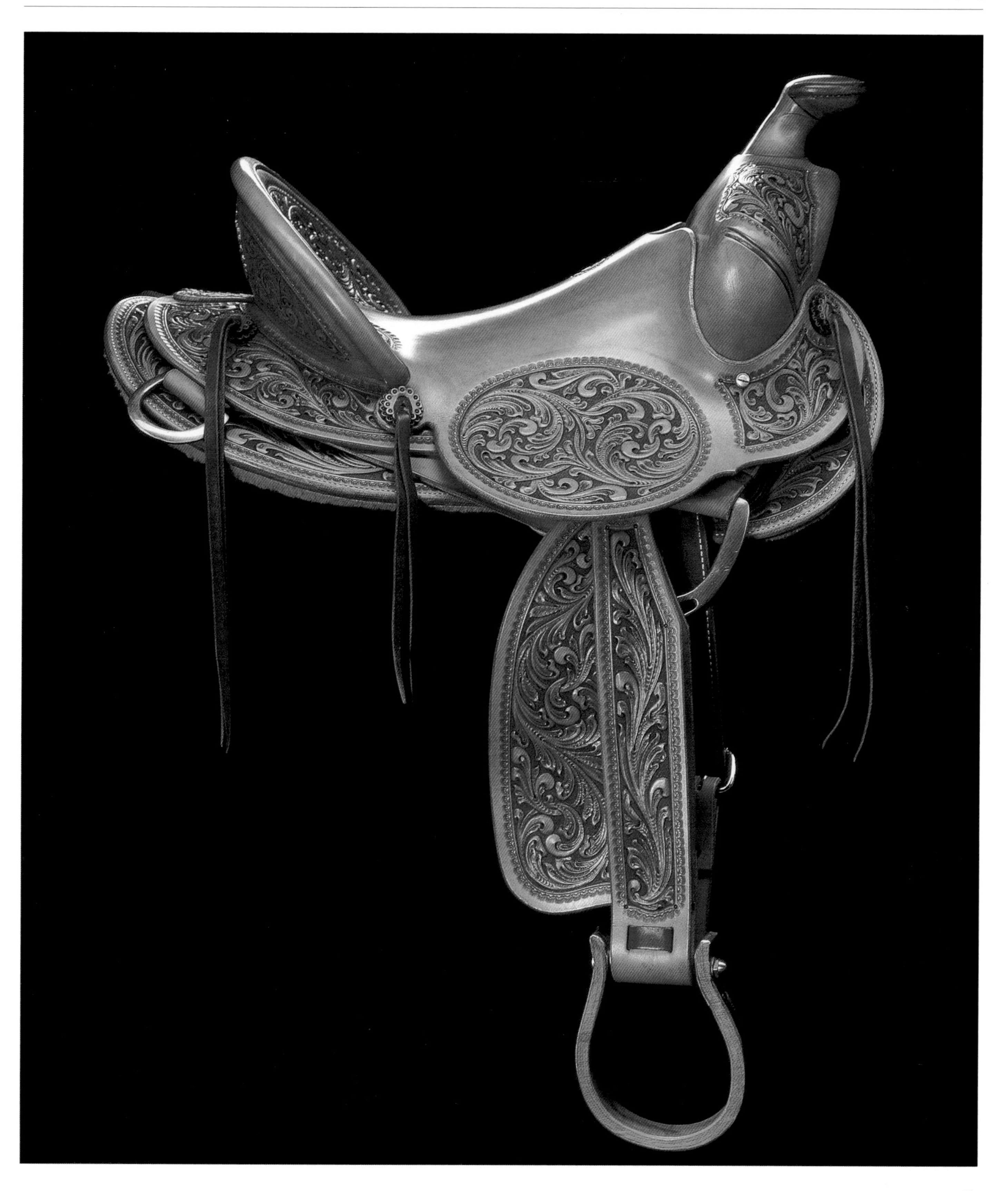

Less is more. A classically understated, elegant Chuck Stormes saddle pays homage to the Visalia style. (Saddle courtesy of D. D. Potter)

CHUCK STORMES

When the Texas cowboys pushed their herds north to the beckoning grasslands of Montana and Wyoming, some of those long-ago stockmen drove their "white man's buffalo" on across the Medicine Line into Canada. Although subjects of the Queen, their true loyalties remained with the cowboy fraternity and the traditions they had carried north.

To service the needs of their Canadian cowboy cousins, saddle makers soon set up shop across Alberta's vast plains and in British Columbia's mountain valleys. In a tradition that endures to this day, Canadian saddles built a reputation for rugged utility like their distant Texas forebears. Of the Canadian makers, the house of Eamor became the most famous. In their northern fastness, however, firms such as Calgary's Riley and McCormack and individual saddlers produced exceptional kacks in relative obscurity, little known below the border.

From this rich heritage, one maker has emerged as the dean of contemporary Canadian saddlery, Chuck Stormes of Calgary, Alberta. In his Stampede City shop, Stormes crafts saddles prized throughout the world, his mastery eclipsing nationality and boundaries. Raised on a ranch east of Calgary, he was strongly influenced by his stepfather, an accomplished horseman. Chuck's love of horses fostered a desire to be a veterinarian. A bright student, Stormes graduated from high school a year early at age sixteen. Unfortunately, college admission policies forbade acceptance of undergraduates younger than seventeen. Left at loose ends, Chuck cast about for something to occupy him for a year. An advertisement in a Calgary newspaper announcing a saddle-making apprenticeship at Riley and McCormack's captured his attention. Reporting for duty, Chuck was apprenticed to John Foss, a veteran of the trade whose own apprenticeship was in the 1880s. By year's end, veterinary medicine was forgotten. Instead of finding a diversion for a year, he had found a calling for a lifetime.

In addition to Foss's mentorship, the Visalia Saddle Company's work also influenced the formative craftsman. Appreciation of Visalia saddles and their makers, such as Dave Silva, has been abiding. Stormes regards the saddles made in the San Francisco Bay area between the World Wars as the trade's zenith. Ray Holes was another hero. During Chuck's early years, the Holes catalogue was always at the workbench providing inspiration.

After mastering the basics through apprenticeship and years of practice, Stormes established his own firm. From his initial Alberta working-cowboy clientele, his customer list has grown to include pleasure riders, showmen and collectors as well. A true NAFTA business,

Stormes ships saddles to virtually all the American states and overseas. During his years in the trade, Stormes has enjoyed a high level of repeat business, a sure indication of customer satisfaction.

Remembering his own beginnings with John Foss, Stormes occasionally took on a student. Jeremiah Watt put in time under Chuck's expert tutelage. Stormes is quick to warn aspiring saddle makers. He reckons it takes ten years of apprenticeship and practice to really master the trade and another ten years building a clientele. To make it as a quality saddle maker, you have to be talented, young, single and an easy keeper. With the cost of trees, skirting leather, sewing machines and tools, starting out isn't for the fainthearted.

Stormes divides saddle making into two related processes: mechanics (the kack's actual construction) and art (the stamping and carving). A good saddle maker excels at one part of the process; a great saddler excels at both. An exceptional mechanic, Stormes prides himself on the seat he puts in a saddle. One of only a few saddlers making their own trees, Chuck has a tremendous advantage in controlling the entire process. Every saddle Stormes makes is constructed as if it were going to be ridden all day, every day, by an Alberta ranch hand.

Reflecting his affinity for the California style, refinement is a word he frequently uses. His skilled hands create saddles that are stronger yet lighter than the coarser rigs of most contemporaries.

Refinement also describes the tooling and carving distinguishing a Stormes creation. His full-flower-stamped saddles are stunning. Thanks to the patronage of collectors and aficionados, he can pursue his passion for fine, elaborate carving and tooling that the average cowboy cannot afford. If artists know fine art, there can be no greater affirmation of Stormes' talent than the fact that Cowboy Artists of America members Joe Beeler and Bill Owens ride Chuck's saddles. When team roping together, they ride functional art, proving that Chuck's masterpieces are for using as well as admiring.

Sometime well into the twenty-first century, Stormes will hand on the tools inherited from Foss. A passing of the torch, another gifted young artisan will continue his passion for quality saddle making. That will be Stormes' ultimate contribution to the art of saddle making.

Refined lines and subtle detailing distinguish Chuck Stormes' work. (Saddle courtesy of D. D. Potter)

Jeremiah Watt

Intense . . . driven . . . fiercely dedicated. These terse summaries by contemporary gear makers capture the essence of Jeremiah Watt. A compelling force, Watt is a driving engine behind the cowboy Trappings movement. A modern-day renaissance man, his impact on the trade is profound. The scope of his contribution as a saddle, bit and spur maker, entrepreneur and impresario is unique.

Perhaps Watt was predisposed to being an artisan. His father was a renowned tinsmith. Though working in different mediums, father and son share a common genius. Classically trained, Jeremiah apprenticed for seven years under the dean of Canadian saddlery, Chuck Stormes. The apprenticeship was comprehensive, covering all aspects of saddlery, including tree making. By contemporary standards, Jeremiah's apprenticeship was long; yet, at its finish, he didn't consider himself an accomplished saddle maker.

A Jeremiah Watt creation featuring elaborate carving and silverwork. (Saddle courtesy of Dary Reed)

To refine his technique and perfect his own style, Watt cast loose from his mentor, drifting south from the land of the Maple Leaf to the buckaroo country of Nevada and California. The change was invigorating. It was a time of artistic foment. The Trappings movement was awakening and Watt was in a hotbed of cowboy culture. Area cowboys appreciated and purchased unique, handcrafted saddles, spurs and bits.

Riding for area ranchers, Watt used saddles and made them, too. Range experience deepened his understanding of building saddles that fit both horse and rider. Watt's time on horseback also brought him in contact with influential trainers such as Buck Brannaman. These relationships were mutually beneficial. Jeremiah gained insight from these experts while they came to appreciate the outstanding quality and beauty of his saddles.

Watt also caught the attention of watercolorist William Matthews, acclaimed painter of contemporary buckaroo life. *Forbes* magazine observed, "The artist who captures the cowboy, captures the American soul. Once it was Frederic Remington. Now it is William Matthews." His painting *Jeremiah Watt* captures a proud, self-confident buckaroo as comfortable in the saddle as at the workbench. One of Matthew's prized possessions, a trophy of his time among the Great Basin buckaroos, is a hand-tooled, silver-trimmed Jeremiah Watt saddle that sits in his studio.

Silver trim expanded Watt's scope as a gear maker. Many customers ordered saddles with ornamentation. Unhappy with the quality of commercially available silverwork, Jeremiah determined he could do better. With characteristic zeal, he threw himself into the project. In short order, he was an accomplished silversmith.

Watt discovered he had an affinity for metalwork. Expanding his repertoire, Jeremiah began to create exceptional California-style bits and spurs. Along with Bill Heisman, Watt is a rare "all arounder" who works both ends of the gear-making arena with virtuosity. In some circles, Watt is now as well known for his bits and spurs as his saddles.

Not content to be a leading light in contemporary western gear making, he has turned his relentless energy to creating new opportunities to showcase quality custom cowboy gear. While many leading artisans find the business side of the trade a necessary evil, to Watt, it is an opportunity. Jeremiah recognizes that a fundamental challenge facing custom gear makers is earning a decent living.

Craftsmen often have a hand-to-mouth existence without steady income or extra funds to set aside for medical insurance or retirement. To address this problem, Watt applies modern business practices, market development, promotion, and cost and production controls to increase sales and profit margins. Some purists find this anathema, as if marketing saddles and spurs with an eye to the bottom line lessens the gear's quality.

Watt's tireless crusade is not self-centered. His promotional and educational activities benefit all western gear makers. Events he has organized, such as the recent "Cowboy Chrome" exhibit of fancy silverwork at the Western Folklife Center in Elko, showcase leading artisans and develop an educated, expanding client base. His seminars and classes provide knowledge and inspiration to future generations of western craftsmen.

Jeremiah's passion for his trade is matched by his passionate devotion to his family. In common with many leading craftsmen, his family is an integral part of his work. His wife, Colleen, is the quintessential western helpmate. An integral part of the business, she makes Jeremiah's prolific output possible. With his fresh approach to the business of making and selling quality, custom working gear, Watt is the future of the trade. By combining the best of the old ways with the realities and opportunities of today, Watt is blazing a bold new trail.

Brass stud work, rawhide bindings, bucking rolls and silver horn cap express Jeremiah Watt's broad creative genius. (Saddle courtesy of Dary Reed)

SCOTT BROWN

Scott Brown's saddle-making odyssey is uncannily similar to that of his mentor, Eddie Brooks. Trained in Texas, both perfected their skills in Nevada at Capriola's. Just as Capriola's owner lured Brooks to Elko to give his firm an injection of fresh insight and vigor, Gary Dunshee, owner of Big Bend Saddlery in Alpine, Texas, brought Brown back to Texas to infuse new perspectives and artistic flair into Lone Star saddle making. The talented Brown was an ideal choice for the mission.

Unique among leading contemporary saddle makers, Brown is a trade-school alumnus. With the proliferation of saddle factories, particularly in Texas, trade school programs have been created to satisfy the demand for employees.

Armed with his diploma and a rudimentary understanding of the trade, Scott signed on at Ryon's, working in their custom order shop. Blessed with natural talent and dedication, he rapidly became a prized employee. Seeking an "ivy league" firm for graduate-level matriculation, he joined Capriola's, where his skills blossomed.

To broaden his experience, Scott abandoned his stool at the workbench for a seat on the hurricane deck. Although he rode a little, Scott didn't call himself a hand. He wanted to know more about using saddles so he could build better ones. Brown loved his sabbatical. He readily took to cowboying, earning his keep riding for top Nevada outfits including the famous Wine Cup. Brown became a full-fledged buckaroo, even frequently serving as a painting subject for watercolorist William Matthews. As handy with fiddle and a bow as a big loop, Scott was also a particular favorite around the campfire.

It was with mixed emotions that Brown returned to saddle making, but his hard-earned experience paid tremendous dividends when he opened his own shop. The importance of a good ground seat and properly set rigging had become painfully clear. Based on experience, Brown can now watch somebody ride and recommend the seat and rigging best suited to his or her build and way of sitting a horse.

Brown's buckaroo days also gave him an appreciation for the value Nevada cowboys place on style. Good looks must complement quality construction if a maker is going to develop a following. Scott strives to build saddles with symmetry of line complemented by attractive carving and stamping. As functional art, Brown's saddles grace the backs of horses in the stable of Waddie Mitchell, cowboy poet laureate. As kinetic sculpture, Scott's saddles grace the William Matthews Gallery in Denver.

While Brown loves making saddles, he is less enthusiastic about running a small business. So, Gary Dunshee's offer to handle the business part of saddle making was especially appealing. As a top saddler, Dunshee appreciates Scott's artistic concerns. Their supportive relationship would not exist if the partnership's goal was based on meeting production schedules and quotas rather than building exceptional saddles.

However, the move from Nevada to Texas meant Scott had to readjust to Texas ways. He now builds different types of saddles reflecting the priorities and working conditions in Texas. Most working saddles in Nevada are elaborately carved and tooled and frequently sport a bit of silver. Texas working saddles tend to be rough outs or have little tooling. As a wag expressed the differences, "In Nevada, buckaroos drive a beat-up old pickup with an expensive, fancy saddle in the back. In Texas, cowboys drive an expensive, shiny pickup with a beat-up old saddle in the back."

Scott has taken up the cause of introducing finely carved saddles like a missionary crusade. He has planted the seed of high-quality craftsmanship in the soil of Texas. Nurtured by Gary Dunshee, his efforts are bearing fruit. With a full order book and growing appreciation of custom saddles, the return of the native has been a happy homecoming.

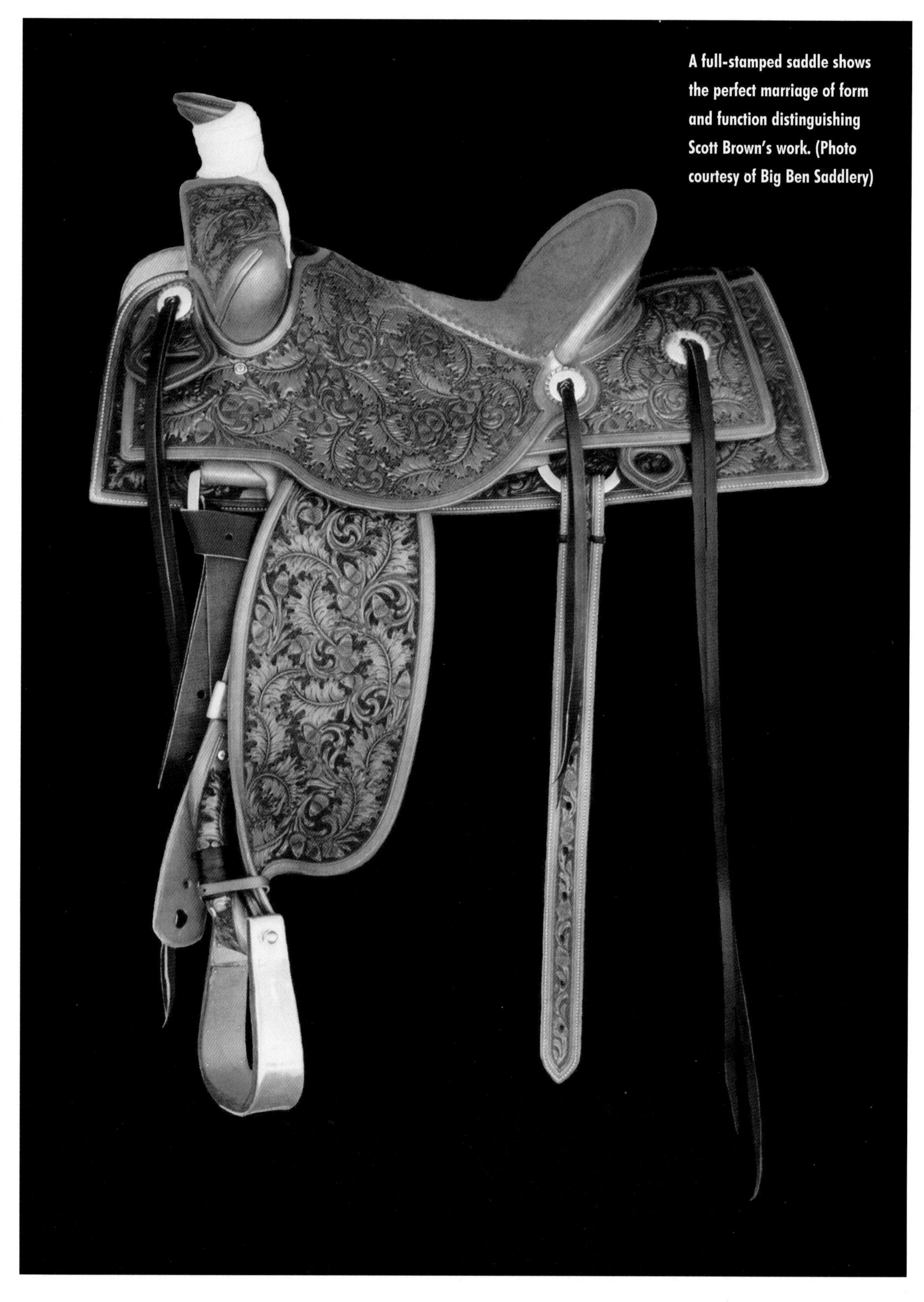

A full-stamped saddle shows the perfect marriage of form and function distinguishing Scott Brown's work. (Photo courtesy of Big Ben Saddlery)

A COWBOY'S HISTORY OF BITS & SPURS

A wag once opined that a cowboy would as soon be seen in public without his spurs as his pants. There is an underlying truth to this remark. Many cowboys are never observed without their spurs. They strap them on a new pair of boots, and the spurs don't come off until the boots are worn out and thrown away.

While the horse wears the saddle and bit, the cowboy wears the spurs. Bestowed with colorful monikers in the cowboy's vernacular lexicon, including "persuaders," "pet makers," "gut hooks" or "Chihuahuas," they are one of the delights in a cowboy's life. Spurs are integral to his self-image and essential to his trade. A pair of custom, handcrafted spurs, often costing a month's wages, represents a major investment for a working cowboy. It is a price gladly paid. A handsome pair of spurs is a badge of identification. Anyone can wear a cowboy hat and boots, but you had better be a real hand if you are going about sporting a pair of "buzz saws." They mark membership in an exclusive brotherhood. Like a Tibetan prayer wheel, the rowels' gentle jangling constantly remind the wearer of who and what he is.

Historically, spurs denoted a mounted, martial nobility. The Spanish *gachupin,* the man on horseback who colonized the New World, epitomized a culture based on the mounted, aristocratic warrior. From atop their horses, they viewed the world with the assured self-confidence of lords of the earth. The spur was the *gachupin's* symbol of office, clearly establishing his rightful primacy in Spanish colonial culture.

As with horses, spurs graphically reflected the power grandees exercised over colonial societies—commanding obedience, compelling action and inflicting punishment. When ruthlessly employed, they were instruments of cruelty and torture. Judiciously applied, spurs communicated resolve, signaled purpose and called forth greater effort.

References to spurs in this capacity are embedded in our language. Coaches "spur" their teams on to greater effort. "Winning your spurs" acknowledges successful completion of a rite of passage. Many a western preacher has delivered a sermon likening a cowboy's use of spurs to get a stubborn horse's attention to God's quickening of a parishioner's hardened conscience.

ARTISTIC STYLE

As with saddles and bits, spurs reflect cowboydom's two schools of style—the Texas-Great Plains persuasion and the brotherhood from California and the Great Basin. Those influenced by the Californios tend to have more ornamentation and larger rowels, make greater use of

Ready for action, a pair of spurs awaits its owner.

The jingle bobs, rowels and heel chains of these Jesse Marsh spurs sound the cadence of the West.

silver, feature intricate inlay work and employ chap guards and jingle bobs. While the California style favors the rococo, Texas spurs could be said to reflect Shaker design principles. Plainer, with shorter, angular shanks, less ornamentation and smaller rowels, their appeal lies in an elegant, understated simplicity. Over time, these geographic distinctions have blurred under the assault of mass production and marketing. The recent resurgence of fine custom-crafted spurs has not only reversed the trend toward homogenized mediocrity but also revived regional peculiarities.

Contemporary spur makers employ several ingredients to "put the pretty" on a pair of spurs, starting with the basic form. Variations in the heel band, spur buttons, shank and rowels provide the artisan with scope for esthetic expression. Once the shape is sketched out, the craftsman has further avenues of creativity in selecting the metals employed to transform the spur from concept to hard-edged reality. Finishes provide the craftsman a broad palette, including glossy and matte blacks, gunmetal blues, soft grays, anodized browns and bronzes, and burnished copper and silver. Then come the embellishments: jingle bobs, chap guards, engraving, and inlays or overlays of gold, silver, bronze or copper.

Silverwork ranges from fine, delicate filigree inlays to bold silhouette overlays. Designs include traditional themes such as moons and stars, floral patterns, the suits of cards, initials, brands, arrows and animals, as well as Islamic crescents and complex Moorish-inspired forms carried to the New World by Spanish colonialists.

Specialization

In addition to more stylized, individualistic custom spurs, increasing specialization influences the work of contemporary makers. Nowhere is this more evident than in the rodeo arena. Rough stock contestants ride with an angled or offset shank, making it easier to "stroke" a violently bucking horse or bull. Even among the crowd found behind the bucking chutes, there are subtle variations between saddle bronc, bareback and bull riders' spurs. Ropers, meanwhile, wear spurs with short, straight, often upturned shanks. This facilitates rapid dismounting without snagging a foot on the saddle and prevents tripping when on the ground. Barrel racers wear lightweight, specially angled "hooks," often constructed without rowels like an English hunting spur.

Outside the rodeo arena, other western competitors wearing specialized spurs include cow cutters, reining horse competitors and team penners. In these competitions, the spur is essentially a communications device, alerting the horse to intended actions.

Strapping on the iron, a bareback rider gets ready to ride.

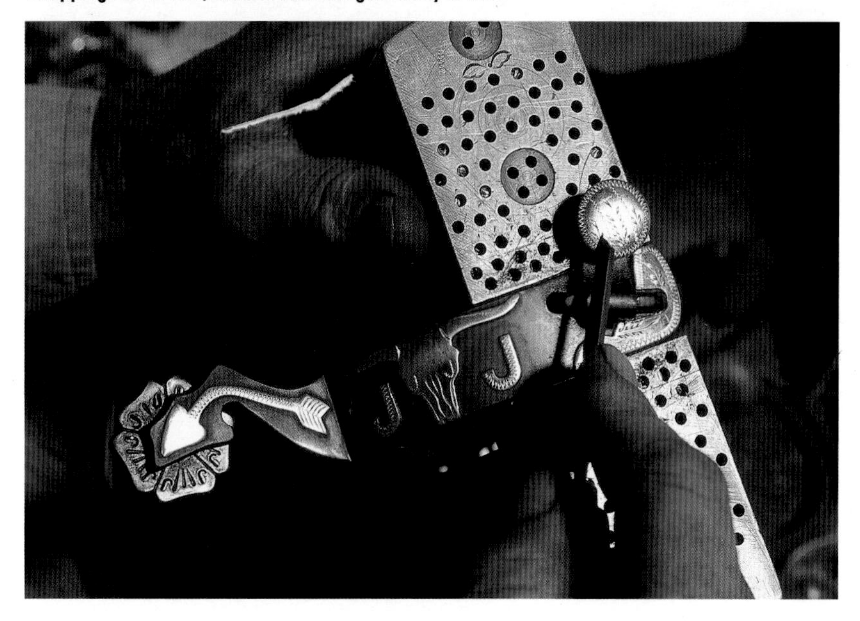

Putting the pretty on a spur, a maker engraves his silverwork.

Music to the Ears

While all good spurs are comfortable to wear and effectively signal the horse of the rider's intentions, great spurs are endowed with a special panache of sight and sound. The spurs' musical attributes are one of their most enduring traits. The lyrics to the song, "Git Along, Little Dogies,"

As I was a walkin' one mornin' for pleasure,
I spied a cowpuncher a-ridin' along,
His hat was throwed back and his spurs were a-jinglin',
And as he approached he was singin' this song

perfectly capture the cowboy's free and easy, open nature. The cadence of the West is sounded by the spurs' gentle jangle, a syncopated symphony of the range starkly contrasting with urban America's strident cacophony.

Recently, the solitary note of a chiming spur has begun to swell to a crescendo as the finest group of spur makers the West has known toil away at forge, anvil and workbench, crafting exceptional spurs. Blessed with the heritage of such "old masters" as Garcia, McChesney and Crockett as a foundation, their successors enjoy the advantages of better, more precise tools; advanced metallurgical technologies; the application of techniques adapted from other disciplines, such as gun engraving; and the stimulation

An ornate, silver-mounted, California-style spade bit by Mark Dahl. (Bit courtesy of Vicky Mullins, Hitching Post Supply)

of frequent interchanges with their fellows. Driven by an inner compulsion that fills them with a single-minded desire for perfection, they constantly strive for improvement. In their quest, today's top makers are refining traditional techniques and themes to jewel-like brilliance while their imagination, creativity and initiative compels them to seek new horizons. Spur makers from the West's first golden age left a legacy of excellence that today's craftsmen perpetuate with new drama and the promise of timelessness.

Bits

Bits are not celebrated in song or poem. Colorful references to them don't salt our language. As a visual symbol, bits cannot compete with saddles or spurs. They go quietly about their business, largely unsung. To members of the cowboy fraternity, however, they are a subject of paramount concern.

Poorly made spurs are an inconvenience. A cheap, ill-fitting saddle may temporarily sore up horse or rider. The wrong bit, wrongly used, can ruin a horse. When a cowboy chooses a bit, he wants an instrument that elicits maximum response from the animal, is easy on its mouth, will survive the beating inflicted on working gear, and possesses eye-catching appeal. Creating such paragons is the province of the master bit maker.

Californio vs. Texican Style

True to form, the two lines of the cowboy's progenitors held markedly different views regarding bits. Texas men and their High Plains cousins favored the plain, simple, light curb or "grazing" bit, so named because its short-shanked cheek piece and simple mouth bar allowed the horse to forage while bitted. Californios and their Great Basin brethren were fanatically devoted to the ornate, complex, heavy spade bit and its close relative, the half-breed. The moniker *spade* recognizes a large, spoon-shaped appendage attached to the mouthpiece. Integral to the mouthpiece is a roller, or "cricket," which the horse rolls with its tongue. Beyond soothing the animal, the cricket produces a clicking sound that appeals to the California crowd's musical ear.

While arguments over the worth of the

rawhide reata compared to the seago lariat or the center-fire saddle's virtues in relation to the full double rig were mostly joshing, discussions of the spade and grazer were laced with venom. Texans and their crowd contemptuously referred to spades as "stomach pumps," "bear traps" or "tool chests," considering them unnecessarily severe. As an old waddie observed, "A spade ain't no kind of bit for a man with a temper." To their view, any horse needing that much hardware in its mouth wasn't much of a horse.

West of the Rockies, use of the spade was regarded as an art form and afforded near-religious reverence. Buckaroos passionately believed that the bit imparted a certain style, a grace of carriage and responsiveness that distinguished a genuine spade horse. To a true devotee, there wasn't a decent moving or reining cow pony east of the Continental Divide. Californios vehemently protested the contention that the spade was cruel. If used properly, they argued, it was actually more humane than low-port curb bits. As they saw it, a grazer-bit man was far more likely to jerk a horse around, damaging its mouth.

The current cowboy revival, fostered primarily by the Nevada buckaroo, has rekindled interest in the spade. Hands are once more committing the time and effort required to develop well-schooled, spade bit horses.

Many non-western horsemen see no merit in either camp's arguments. They regard all western bits—grazers, half-breeds and spades—as harsh and cruel. In theory, they are right. A western bit in the hands of the ignorant or bullheaded can inflict severe damage to a horse's tender mouth. A good horseman, however, does not ride on his horse's mouth. Rather, he rides with a loose rein, turning the horse by laying the rein against its neck and stopping or backing the animal with light pressure on the reins. A mark of a true cowboy is the ability to train and ride velvet-mouthed horses with a light hand.

Born in fire, a bit is milled to aerospace tolerances.

Tradition Meets Technology

Today's makers work within the stream of tradition, its headwaters tracing back to the fountainhead of seminal masters. Such legendary makers as Kelly and Crockett set the standard for the finest Texas-style bits while their counterparts, Garcia and Morales, made the mark for California-type spades and half-breeds. While contemporary bit makers perpetuate the broad regional styles associated with Texas and California, they bring fresh insight, inspiration and technological innovation to the trade. They enjoy the advantages of advances in metallurgy, tools and equine sciences as well as the ability to draw from the well of accumulated knowledge. Cumulatively, these developments allow current artisans to make bits of greater quality, utility and beauty than those of the founding fathers. This is not to disparage the work of old-time makers. Remarking on the advantages today's craftsmen enjoy, a leading bit maker observed, "If the power goes out, I'm out of business."

Contemporary bit making demands expertise in diverse disciplines. The craftsman must possess a working knowledge of metallurgy,

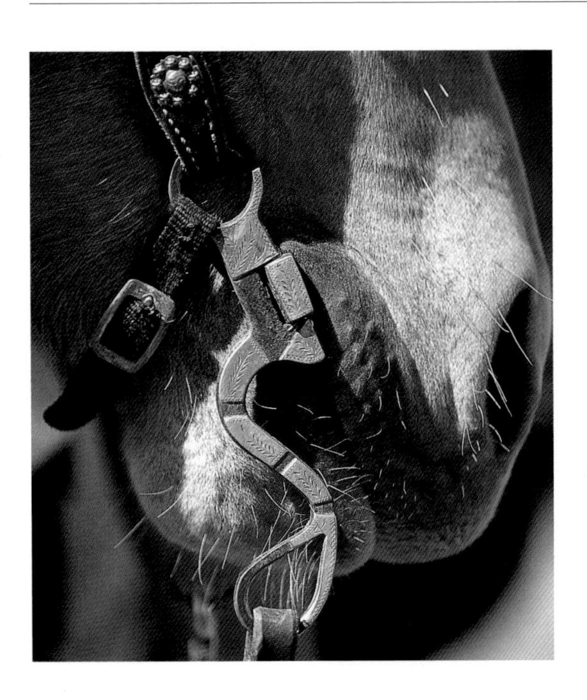

Still eye-catching after years of hard use, this bit is perfectly at home in a horse's mouth.

physics, anatomy and equine psychology. Many excellent spur makers do not create bits because they are complex and time-consuming. It is easier to sell a pair of fancy spurs than a finely crafted bit. Reviewing his order book, a top bit-and-spur maker noted that he currently has deposits for fifty pairs of spurs but only four bits. Many artisans create bits for the technical challenge and the close working relationship they foster with serious horsemen as much as for the financial reward.

The bit maker must be a master metalworker, able to forge and weld materials with finite precision. A rough weld or burr will irritate a horse's mouth, distracting the mount from its work. The canons, the outer portion of the mouthpiece, must be painstakingly built up and machined to aerospace tolerances to fit comfortably on the bars of the mouth. Bits require absolute symmetry. Just as a car out of alignment will not steer properly, a crooked bit does not hang true and applies pressure unevenly to the horse's mouth.

The great bit maker is a metallurgist, appreciative of metals and their properties. Different metals are better suited to certain types or parts of bits. Understanding a metal's epicurean potential in creating a mild, or sweet-tasting, mouthpiece marks an expert. A horse will gladly accept a sweet, saliva-producing mouthpiece, happily carrying it all day. A bitter, harsh-tasting bit will have the opposite effect, making a horse hard to bridle and distracted in its work.

A practical appreciation of the laws of physics is required. Makers must calculate the torque generated on the mouthpiece by the leverage of the cheek-piece shank. The longer the length and straighter the angle of the shank, the greater the leverage. Failure to properly balance the bit, compensating for these forces, will place too much pressure on the bars or cause the bit to turn over in the horse's mouth.

Building a good bit requires more than a nodding acquaintance with equine anatomy. To understand how the bit interacts with the animal, it is important to know the physical structure and processes within the horse's mouth. For all its tenderness, the horse's mouth is a hostile environment, producing corrosive salts, acids and rusting moisture.

The workings of the horse's mind also come into play. Empathy with the factors that soothe or agitate a horse contributes to building bits that maximize performance. No bit works on every horse. Selecting the proper bit to suit the horse is often more a matter of disposition than physical structure. The human mind also comes into play. Bits are not selected or used in a vacuum. They must suit the temperament and riding style of the cowboy purchasing them.

Aesthetic Expression

When the master bit maker settles in at the bench, he is dealing with a limited number of components. Minus snaffles, all western bits share common parts: side or cheek pieces joined by a bit bar or mouthpiece. When viewed from the front, they create the bit's characteristic H shape. Within these functional confines, the artisan enjoys scope for infinite variation. Shape, size and materials afford opportunity for experimentation and expression. Shapes run the gamut from stolid solidity to sensuous curves to elegant contemporary lines. From the large, heavy, Santa Barbara spade bit to the barely there snaffle, size is a variable related to function and the maker's whim. Bits are forged or cast from iron, steel, brass, bronze, copper or aluminum, singly or in combination. Function, price and personal preference play a role in determining the materials employed. As a medium of expression, the bit's cheek pieces allow the craftsman to let loose the muse of artistic display.

With a characteristic crescent shape forged in the cheek piece and intricate inlaid silverwork, the Santa Barbara-style bit pays homage to its Islamic origin. Set beneath a circular "full moon" form, the crescent also marks a celestial tribute to the phases of the moon. Sentimental hearts and flowers adorn many cheek pieces. The perennial cowboy favorites—heart, club, spade and diamond—are well represented. One could populate a bestiary with the creatures found on cheek pieces—slithering snakes, rearing horses, howling coyotes, fluttering birds, rampant bears, lowering buffalo, strutting peacocks, slippery fish and trumpeting swans. The female form is well represented in different types of "gal leg" and full-figure poses.

The artisan complements the bit's form with a variety of finishes. Matte or glossy jet blacks, soft French or gunmetal grays, flashy blues, anodized browns or bronzes, glowing brasses, and gleaming silvers and coppers provide an expansive palette. Form and finish are complemented by a broad range of adornment. While copper and brass are used, silver is a crowning glory on most fine bits. It can be found as domed buttons, conchos, intricately engraved inlays or simple, bold overlays. In the opinion of noted western chronicler Jo Mora, when it came to bits, "nothing is handsomer than good silverwork with the background of brown steel." Today, he would find that top hands still share that opinion. With a marriage of utility-driven form and decorative embellishment, bits epitomize functional art.

Silverwork, engraving and a matte French gray finish distinguish the work of Ernie Marsh.

Though each bit maker shares the common goal of producing a good using, eye-catching bit, they are individualists with their own thoughts, ideas, skills and experience applied in their own particular way. Ingeniously combining age-old concepts with emerging technologies, these artisans employ imagination, creativity and initiative to expand the craft's horizons. They are creating new traditions with the richness of yesterday and vitality of today that promise to be the masterpieces of tomorrow.

SPUR MAKERS

JERRY VALDEZ

Jerry Valdez's transition from rodeo cowboy to top spur maker followed a trail familiar to many leading artisans. Bitten by the rodeo bug, education was a secondary concern as he was growing up. The scores that mattered were for bareback riding, not SATs. When your parents are university professors, this can present a problem. Encouraged by his father, he agreed to enroll in a college metallurgy program while competing in the PRCA.

As a class project, he made a pair of spurs, improving on the buzz saws he rode with. The class project earned the admiration of fellow competitors. Soon he was making spurs for other rough stock riders, spurs as tough as the men who wear them and the stock they ride.

Cowboys using Valdez spurs to "scratch" their way to the pay window comprise a "Who's Who" of the rodeo world. Among their number are All-Around Champion Louis Fields, two-time Bareback Gold Buckle winner Wayne Herman, and many time National Finals Qualifiers Cody Lambert, Tommy Reeves and Mel Coleman. Additionally, Rodeo Hall of Fame stock contractor Harry Vold and his son, NFR pickup man and recording artist, Wayne, strap on Jerry's steel.

While long on using, his early bronc spurs weren't much for looks. Jerry considered himself a metal bender, not a silversmith. The transition to fancier spurs began more by chance rather than design. Valdez agreed to make a pair of spurs with silver initials. Too green to realize what he was getting into, Jerry quoted a price of $75 and figured he was in for a good payday.

A jeweler in Great Falls quoted a price of $25 to make the initials. Jerry figured he was getting a pretty good deal, until the jeweler clarified he meant $25 per letter. Stunned, Valdez asked if there wasn't a cheaper alternative. Half in jest, the jeweler replied, "I could sell you the silver and you could do it yourself." Thus was born Jerry Valdez's career as a silversmith.

Always interested in painting and sculpture, Jerry began to explore the artistic potential of decorated spurs. He was particularly fascinated by the challenge of applying jewelry-design principles to his work.

Jerry's spurs are distinctive, exhibiting a sense of humor and traces of Art Nouveau influences. Bold and clean, his patterns effectively use the spur's plain matte background and the depth of the overlay to create visual excitement and drama. Valdez also explores the use of other precious metals, such as gold, in overlay work.

Jerry's spurs have traveled far from their Montana birthplace. His work has been featured in the Trappings of America show in Flagstaff, Arizona; The Trappings of Texas show in Alpine, Texas; the Western Folklife Center in Elko, Nevada; and the C. M. Russell Museum in Great Falls, Montana. Jerry's spurs were included in an exhibit of western gear that toured Malaysia, Singapore and Thailand. Many top rodeos in Canada and the States, including the Montana PRCA Circuit Finals, award Valdez spurs as prizes. Keeping his hand in rodeo circles, Valdez is a founding member of the PRCA Artists Association and displays his wares at the NFR in Las Vegas, Nevada.

Today, Jerry is thankful for his father's encouragement to pursue the trade seriously and seek a supporting education. Over the years, his brother and now his young daughter have helped Valdez in his shop, making it a family business. This is an aspect of the trade that Jerry treasures. In an ultimate irony, Jerry's father now helps in the shop on occasion to help keep up with demand, an affirmation of the adage that sometimes father does know best.

Art Nouveau, 24-carat moons and stars grace these Jerry Valdez spurs.

Tough as the men who wear them and the horses they ride, this pair of Kelly Wardell spurs are made from a horse-shoeing rasp. (Spurs courtesy of Larry Sandvick)

KELLY WARDELL

If you called central casting and said, "Send me the archetype cowboy," chances are he would look like Kelly Wardell. Lanky, rawhide tough and ruggedly handsome, Kelly looks like what he is: one of the PRCA's top bareback riders. In 1994, he was on track to qualify for the NFR in Las Vegas, Nevada. Rodeo's Super Bowl and World Series, it is the goal of all the sport's competitors. At the Pike's Peak or Bust Rodeo in Colorado Springs, Wardell felt a searing pain as he spurred his horse out. He had ripped a groin muscle. The ride, and Wardell's dream year, came to a crashing end.

Missing the Finals was a bitter disappointment. Not only had his life's dream turned to dust, Kelly had to face the pressing reality of earning a living while his injuries healed. Unlike other professional athletes, rodeo cowboys don't have a paid injured reserve. For them, it's compete or you don't eat.

During his enforced exile from rodeo, Kelly returned to his hometown of Moorcroft, Wyoming, to try his hand at making spurs. Located in the state's harsh, sparsely settled northeast corner, Moorcroft is a real western town—the kind of place where a person has to turn his hand to just about anything to survive, not a gentrified and romanticized vision of the West like Cody or Jackson Hole. In his *Wyoming Handbook,* Don Pitcher says of the town, "It isn't particularly attractive, but it will do as a stop on the way to somewhere else."

For Wardell, it was a stop until he could get back on the rodeo road. Although he had never made a pair of spurs and lacked formal metalwork training, Wardell had often helped his father in the family ranch's machine shop. Kelly had spent a good deal of time—something rodeo cowboys have a lot of while traveling the long, lonely roads between shows—thinking about the spurs he wanted to make.

His rough stock riding experience gave Kelly the insight to know what a good spur should be. His time in the family machine shed gave Wardell the technical skill to make them and his ingenuity led him to the perfect material from which to craft his spurs. Settled at the workbench, Kelly joined a long succession of working cowboy craftsmen.

When the West was still young, it was not uncommon for a ranch hand to find himself whiling away a long winter's day in the barn punching a forge and anvil rather than little dogies. If the nearest blacksmith was many snow-covered miles away, a cowboy who was a little handy would find himself pressed into duty repairing ranch wagons or farm implements. With the real work done, many of these dragooned smithies tried their hand at fashioning bits or spurs out of pieces of scrap.

Kelly Wardell directly descends from this legacy of working cowboys crafting bits and spurs from recycled materials. His spurs are reincarnations of worn horseshoeing rasps.

Kelly's bronc spurs fit comfortably and securely, are well balanced and facilitate effective spurring. They are also incredibly strong. To date, no one has managed to damage a pair of Kelly's spurs and not for want of trying. He could market his wares with the slogan, "Can't bend 'em, break 'em or shake 'em."

Noted wearers of Wardell competition spurs are World Champion Bareback Rider Clint Cory, many-time National Finals Qualifier Larry Sandvick, rising star Mark Gomes and Canadian standout Darrell Cholach. Kelly's spurs are enjoying increased popularity outside the arena as well. Hands use them in everyday ranch work, and they are held in particularly high regard for use in breaking colts.

Built primarily for strength and practicality in the rodeo arena and on the ranch, Wardell's spurs have an understated visual appeal accentuated by the residual pattern left when the rasp's teeth are ground away. Like many other craftsmen who began by producing strictly utilitarian gear, Kelly has recently begun putting decorative touches such as chap guards, raised shanks and decorative rowels on his spurs. Despite the added flair, at heart they remain good, honest, working spurs for working cowboys.

Ready for a rank one, Kelly Wardell prepares to mount his bareback during his successful drive to the 1996 NFR.

BIT AND SPUR MAKERS

ROBERT CAMPBELL

Texas is a cradle of cowboy civilization. The Brazos and Pecos were fountainheads from which styles and fashions east of the Rockies flowed. Heirs to a rich tradition, Texans take cowboying seriously. Their approach to the trade is direct, practical and without affectation. Texas working gear reflects this no-nonsense, blue-collar style. Saddles, bits and spurs tend to the plain and solid, intended more for use than show. Texans, however, are not plain folk—latter-day secular Shakers or mounted Mennonites renouncing all forms of ornamentation. In moderation and discreetly understated, they fancy a touch of silver and graceful line.

Working within the bounds of traditional styles developed by founding fathers Kelly and Crocket, Robert Campbell and his son, Leo, are refining and reinterpreting their simple, basic tenets with fresh insight and flair. A disciple of

The bronze-brown finish and bold silver overlays of Campbell spurs have instant appeal for working cowboys.

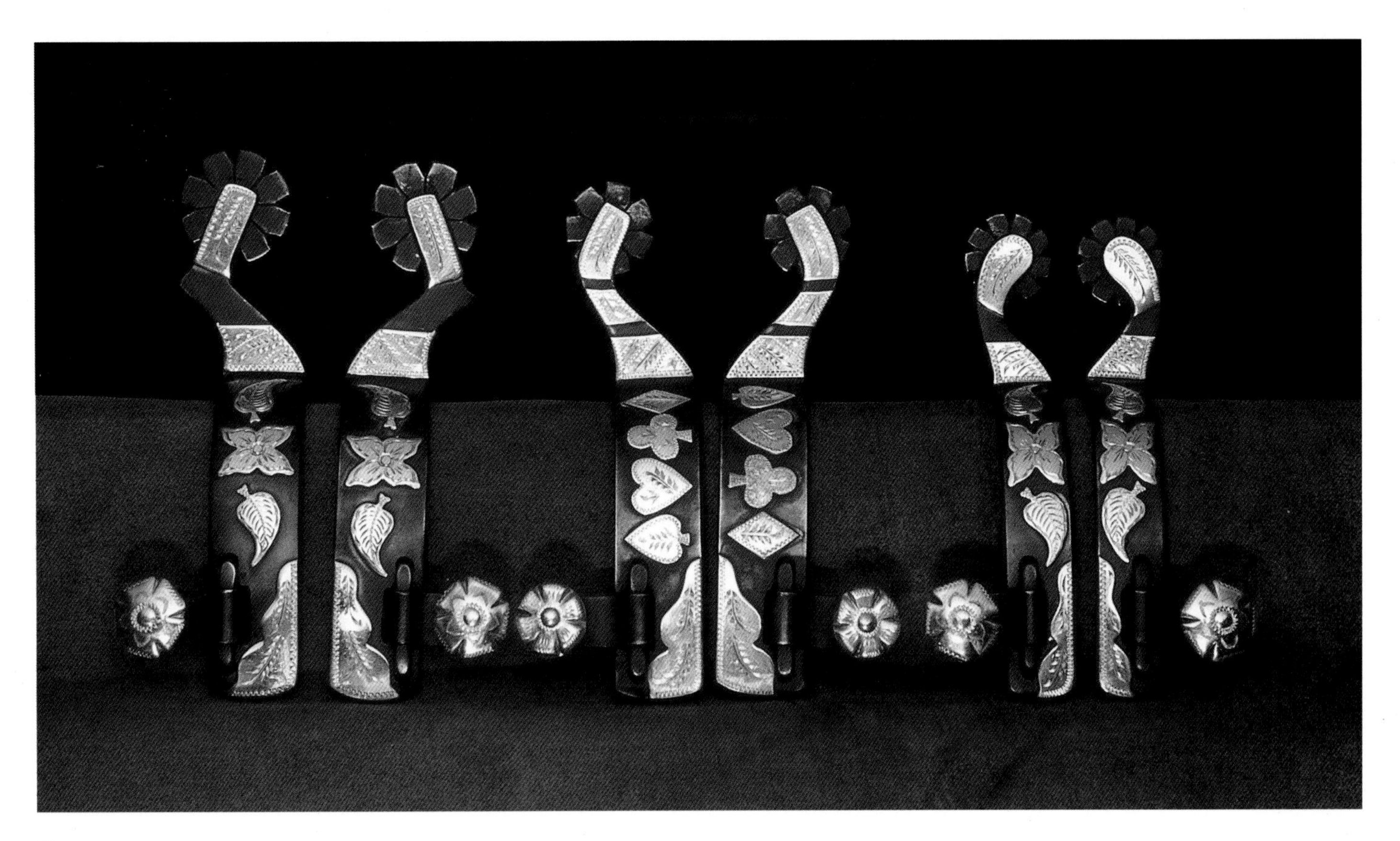

fellow Amarillo artisan Jerry Cates, Robert counts him as a good friend and an inspiration. Campbell strives to model his business after Cates'. This extends to more than the quality and artistry of his work. More importantly, Campbell admires the integrity and gentlemanly manner Cates brings to his dealings. Robert has followed the Cates approach: "build the best quality item you can, sell it to cowboys to use and let the gear talk for itself."

The concept has worked for Campbell, who has logged a dozen years earning a living making bits and spurs full time. Before taking up the trade, Robert was a working ranch cowboy. For a late-twentieth-century top hand, being handy with the welding torch and tool kit are nearly as important as roping and riding. Talented with these new tools of the trade, Robert frequently found himself fixing windmills and repairing broken machinery as often as handling stock.

Short on cash but long on metalworking talent, when Campbell needed some new bits he just went out to the shop and made a couple.

Great looking and a good using bit, this is one of the Campbells' favorites.

Plighting their troth the western way, NFR Pickup Man Randy Hoffman and Champion Barrel Racer Nicole Hoffman exchanged matching Campbell spurs as wedding gifts.

Other cowboys who saw them liked his homemade bits. Soon, Campbell was making simple grazing bits for friends in his spare time. Tough as nails, they were fabricated from cold-rolled steel, a practice he still follows. Contrary to the opinion of some traditionalists who swear by mild-steel mouthpieces, Campbell believes that heating and welding alter the steel's molecular content, sweetening it. With a little copper added, horses take to his mouthpieces like candy.

Growing tired of going broke cowboying, Robert figured he could make a better living working hot irons other than the branding kind. He started a business building welded pipe fencing and made a few bits on the side. Adding spurs to his repertoire, they soon enjoyed the same popularity as his bits. By 1983, a transformation had occurred. Bit and spur making had become his primary focus with fence building relegated to a sideline. Enjoying the former far more than the latter, Robert became a full-time gear maker.

With natural talent, the influence of Jerry Cates and his own prescription for making good gear, "work, work, work," Campbell's business grew. By 1990, he was able to take on his son, Leo. Working together day in, day out, they are as much friends as father and son.

Together, they have established a distinctive

style. The Campbell look is hard, cold-rolled steel finished with a bronze-brown patina. The color is achieved through application of Plum Brown Barrel Finish, a product primarily used in finishing the barrels of black powder muzzle-loading rifles. The aged look achieved by this process is popular with Lone Star cowboys. This is an important asset, for Campbell notes, "They still put new stuff in the horse trough in Texas." Leo and Robert use their bronze-brown patina to set off bold western silhouettes of longhorns, Texas stars, barbwire, tomahawks, arrowheads and brands. Enhanced with engraving, they make a dramatic statement.

The Campbells are also innovators, designing new bit patterns. They enjoy trying to create items that are "original and really unique." Their spur-pattern bits with cheek pieces shaped like spur shanks and reins that attach via slotted rowels are pretty to look at yet still great using bits. World-famous roper Roy Cooper was so taken with his spur bit that he had one made for his good friend, George Strait.

A veritable cowboy's "Who's Who" use Campbell gear. In addition to Strait and Cooper, other noted clients include Walt Garrison, Ty Murray, Clint Johnson, Tee Woolman, Rich Skelton, Dee Picket and D. J. Johnson. All are repeat customers and walking billboards for Campbell Bit and Spur. The combination of unique good looks, high quality, great utility and reasonable prices are irresistible to working cowboys.

Not content to rely totally on others to showcase the virtues of their wares, the Campbells use them as well. Dab hands, both are good horsemen and tough team and steer ropers. Robert stands among the leaders of the senior steer-roping standings while Leo holds his own at PRCA rodeos. Roping at big shows like the Cheyenne Frontier Days and Dodge City provide ideal field demonstrations.

In addition to word of mouth and rodeo arenas, the Campbells have exhibited their gear at the Elko Cowboy Poetry Gathering, the Western Heritage Classic in Abilene, Texas, the Trappings of Texas Show at Alpine, Texas, and the NFR's Cowboy Christmas trade show. The message must be getting out. At last count, Robert had shipped bits and spurs to thirty-eight states and six foreign countries, proving that the Texas style is popular far beyond the Lone Star state's borders.

Texans may be set in their ways and slow to change their views on cowboying. Some would say they are hidebound. Change, however, does happen deep in the heart of Texas. Just as over time, "Don't mess with Texas" has become the state's contemporary battle cry rivaling "Remember the Alamo," Campbell's may join Kelly's as the popular Texas synonym for spurs.

Bill Heisman

A rare artisan, Bill Heisman is equally gifted as a saddler and bit and spur maker. His eighth birthday present was a set of leather-working tools. While experimenting with tooling and stamping, he got a practical grounding in cowboying, riding for ranches near Tucson, Arizona.

Like many a western youth, Bill tried rodeoing, an experience contributing to his eventual emergence as a bit and spur maker. Bill's brother was extremely strong, so powerful he often bent his spurs. With little money to buy replacements, Bill made their spurs out of necessity. Heisman may be the only bronc rider to have made his own saddle and spurs.

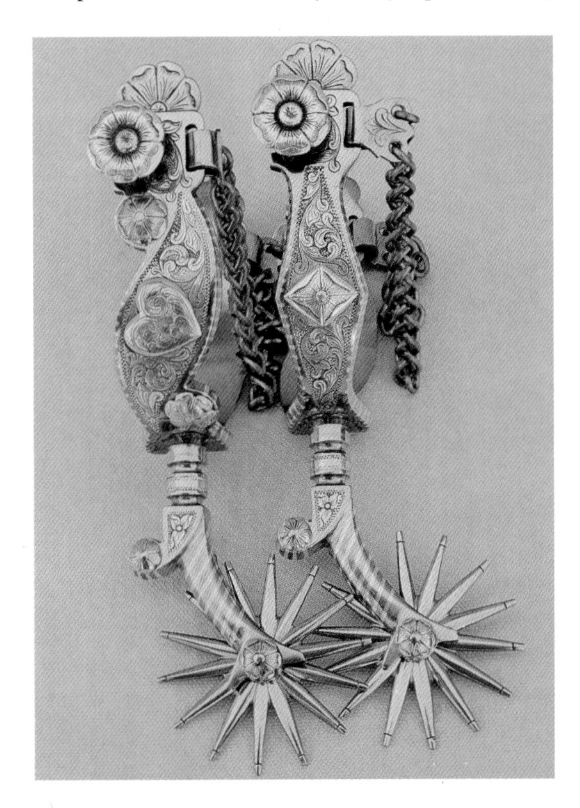

Beneath their beauty, Bill Heisman's bits and spurs have a working heart. (Photo courtesy of Robert Heisman)

With his rodeo days behind him, Bill turned to saddle making as a living. While saddlery was his first love, he harbored a continuing interest in spurs, occasionally making a pair to sell or give to cowboy friends. Living in New Mexico, Heisman was in the Texas sphere of influence but personally preferred the more elaborate California-style bits and spurs.

To further his knowledge, Heisman enrolled in the Miller Bit and Spur School. This training opened new vistas of technique and design concepts. Returning home, Bill's talent and creativity blossomed.

Moving back to Tucson, Heisman has been influenced by the work of Old Mexico's master artisans. Employing techniques closer to the mission artisans of Alta California than the high-tech shops of leading American craftsmen, Bill feels their work is not fully appreciated.

While making all types of pet makers, Heisman's trademark silver-filigree spurs are intricate masterworks coveted by collectors worldwide. Exactingly constructed, the elaborate patterns are painstakingly hand cut with a jeweler's saw and the interstices meticulously chiseled out. With infinite precision, Bill assembles the components employing internal tabs and flawless silver soldering. Elaborately engraved and polished to gemlike brilliance, they are objects of beauty. Like a Fabergé egg, Heisman's spurs are labor intensive, time-consuming creations. A regular pair of buzz saws take a week to make, while Heisman invests a month's time in a filigree set.

Proving just how popular Bill's work is, a recent Trappings of the American West show in Flagstaff resembled the Oklahoma Land Rush. When the doors to the exhibit hall opened, eager collectors sprinted like Sooners to the display cases, vying to be the lucky one to lay claim to a Heisman masterpiece. Within minutes, red "sold" dots decorated every one of his displayed pieces.

Despite acclaim for his spurs, Heisman finds great personal satisfaction in crafting bits. As a working cowboy, Heisman appreciates their importance to the trade. As a skilled craftsman, he appreciates the technical challenge of making them. As an artist, he loves the opportunity to decorate them.

Unfortunately, he doesn't make as many bits as he would like. A review of his order book revealed orders for fifty pairs of spurs compared to four bits. Heisman attributes this disparity to the demand for spurs among collectors. To most people, he says, "spurs and six guns are the West." To serious horsemen, however, bits matter.

He particularly enjoys creating spades because of their associated tradition and lore. Also, they pose a greater technical challenge. Heisman acknowledges the mentorship of California artisan Bob Hall, who helped him master the genre's complexities.

Heisman is not as concerned with detailed metallurgical analysis of a bit's content as some contemporaries. He recalls one of the greatest bit makers he knew swearing by the jack handle of a Ford truck for making sweet mouthpieces. Despite his fierce commitment to functional utility, all of his bits are beautiful objects. Gracefully designed with intricately engraved silverwork, they are equally at home on a den wall or in a horse's mouth.

In recent years, Heisman has become more noted for his silverwork than saddle making. Bill still enjoys leather working, attributing much of his bit and spur success to the freshening change of pace it provides. His exquisite leather work skill graces the spur leathers and headstalls complementing his spurs and bits.

Heisman's vigor and enthusiasm are bolstered by the participation of his son and daughter who are helping him in the shop. Already showing a flair for leather and metalworking, they have the potential for creating a dynasty. Like the Fabergés serving the Russian czars, the Heismans may be creating jewel-like tools of the trade for generations of cowboys yet to come.

Bill Heisman fashioned his trademark filigree spurs with jeweler-like artistry. (Photo courtesy of Robert Heisman)

Cowboy chrome. This snaffle bit is as practical as it is pretty. (Bit courtesy of George and Pidge Ash)

JERRY GINN

Most western gear makers came to their craft early in life. It is a calling, a quest followed with single-minded devotion. Jerry Ginn became a bit and spur maker by fate. Creating western gear opened a new trail, allowing him to continue living the cowboy life when another path dead-ended.

Nevada-born Ginn was destined to be a buckaroo. He grew up cowboying until an invitation from Uncle Sam interrupted his plans. Discharged from the Marine Corps in California, Jerry stayed on in the Golden State working in the glazing business. The pay was good and he had a natural affinity for the work.

The lure of the range, however, proved irresistible, drawing him back to the Nevada ranch country. In his early thirties he was back in the saddle again, riding for ranches in California, Montana and Idaho until a ranching accident shattered his dreams. Severely injured, Jerry realized his days of rough-and-tumble work with cow outfits were over.

Ginn found enforced idleness maddening; he needed something to do. A friend had attended the Miller Bit and Spur School, piquing Ginn's interest in the subject, so Jerry enrolled to learn the basics. With a practical understanding of working gear from his cowboy days and metalworking experience as a glazier, Ginn readily took to the trade.

It didn't take Jerry long to realize that he needed to know a lot more than the basics. To improve his skills, he sought out master artisans, including California bit and spur maker Robert Hall. To improve his engraving skills, Jerry signed on at a school taught by Benno Heune, of Modesto, California. Ginn credits his development as an artisan to this experience. He spent long hours in his shop applying principles and concepts to cold, hard steel. He is adamant that there is no substitute for practice and learning by doing. Progress came rapidly as he refined his technique and developed a distinctive style.

Kooskia, Idaho, was an ideal setting for an aspiring bit and spur maker. It is real cowboy country where fine gear is appreciated. Kooskia is also home to leading artisans such as rawhide braiders and leather workers George and Pidge Ash and their son Harv. Ginn was immersed in a culture that prized quality and stimulated his artistic efforts.

Trained in the California style, Ginn's specialty is crafting mission-style bits and buckaroo spurs. Sporting elaborately forged shanks and intricate, fanciful rowels, and emblazoned with extensive, finely engraved silver inlay work, his spurs are real eye dazzlers. They are finished with a distinctive, antiqued brown patina. Ginn goes the extra mile in detailing his spurs, lavishing attention on subtle extra touches.

Jerry finds that, working with cowboys, strength and durability as well as cost are important factors. Still a working cowboy at heart himself, they are an important clientele to Ginn. True to his cowboy heart, the ring of his spurs matters. Like a composer searching for the lost chord, Ginn experiments with shank and rowel combinations and metal composition, seeking the perfect sound.

Stylish, silver-mounted, California-style spurs are a Jerry Ginn specialty.

Making primarily traditional-style bits, he finds it difficult to improve on what the old-timers did, particularly in size and balance, which they "pretty well worked out." Competing against the work of the masters with knowledgeable horsemen as the arbiters provides a real challenge.

Inventory is the other great challenge Ginn faces. Since taking up the trade, he has sold virtually everything he makes as soon as it is finished. This limits his exposure. In 1995, he participated in the Trappings of the American West show for the first time. True to form, his bits and spurs sold within minutes on the exhibit's opening night. It's a problem many others wish they had.

An innovative and glowing example of the Hayes family work.

THE HAYES FAMILY

The high-stakes, high-pressure world of cutting and reining competition with its hired-gun trainers seems far removed from the workaday world of ranch hands riding the lonesome plains or mesquite thickets. The skills required in these events, however, are firmly rooted in the cowboy's raison d'etre—working cattle on horseback. Performance is essential when thousands of dollars, reputations and egos are on the line.

When demanding owners and trainers of cutting and reining horses seek out high-performance bits and spurs, they frequently turn to the Hayes family of Atascadero, California. The Hayeses—Gordon, Colleen and their son, Wade—combine traditional family values with traditional cowboy gear. In their quarter century in the business, they have developed a loyal following among working cowboys and cutting- and reining-horse people.

The Hayeses grew up ranching and showing horses. After graduating from Cal Poly, the Harvard of agricultural colleges, Gordon and Colleen trained horses as a living. Having worked with many of the Golden State's leading horsemen, they had impeccable credentials. Starting out, times were lean. With little money to buy equipment, Gordon made his own. His unique combination of mechanical talent and horsemanship resulted in well-made and attractive bits and spurs that drew praise from other horse people. Gordon and Colleen decided to see if the compliments could be translated into cash. They made up a batch of bits to sell at a Santa Rosa cutting. Over the weekend, they made $800, which seemed like a fortune to the young couple.

Buoyed by their success, they plunged into the business. Initially, Gordon also made old-style Spanish bits but eventually moved exclusively to more contemporary competition gear. This reflected not only personal preference but also a business decision. Simply put, cutting and reining people had money. It is a hobby for doctors, lawyers and brokers as well as a passion for well-heeled traditional ranching folks.

Much of the Hayeses' early success was associated with the Argentine snaffle. They helped popularize it in competitive circles. Today it remains one of their best-selling bits. Not content to rest on their laurels, Gordon and Wade spend a great deal of time researching metals and new fabrication techniques and experimenting with new designs. Close consultation with their customers provides ideas for improvements and innovations. Each year, they add a few new designs to their inventory, trying not to copy the work of other makers but to reinterpret an earlier concept.

The enduring appeal of Hayes bits and spurs is built on experience-based performance, durability and style. Colleen proudly points out "they are made to last forever." In twenty-five years they have done very little repair work. A troubling trend, observed by other makers as well, is an increasing number of items sent in for repair that are poorly made off-shore knockoffs. In the age of the global village, cheap copies are an unfortunate fact of the craftsman's life.

Flash is an essential component of cutting and reining gear. Elegant lines and silverwork complement the horse and rider, framing their movement. A beautiful bit and spur captures the eye and focuses attention. Set against backgrounds of deep jet or matte black or inking blue, Gordon's silverwork is strikingly attractive. His finishes create a perfect foil showcasing the silverwork, not competing with it. In a variation on the traditional trophy buckle, the Hayeses also make beautiful steel stirrups adorned with silver filigree work, brands or initials. They are prized by fortunate winners.

To sell their gear, family members attend eight to ten cuttings a year, traveling as far as Texas. They also attend snaffle-bit futurities, mixing business with pleasure, for Gordon still trains and rides snaffle horses. Additionally, they sell by mail order and display their wares at the NFR trade show.

A dazzling pair of Hayes spurs. The silverwork contrasts dramatically against a jet finish.

The Hayeses are proud of the business they have built. While they may not be getting rich in the conventional sense, the Hayeses are amassing what are to them more important treasures: the joy of family, being among people they like, and riding every day.

Matching spurs and spade bit showcase Ernie Marsh's engraving skills.

Ernie Marsh

John Day, Oregon, a real cowboy town, guards the northern approaches to Great Basin buckaroo country. It is far removed in more than distance from the moist, forested western slopes of Washington's Cascade Mountains where Ernie Marsh grew up. When Ernie moved to John Day, he found not only a home to his liking but a local culture that nurtured his chosen trade, bit and spur making.

Child of a rodeo family, Ernie was a handy bull rider. To support his weekend habit, Marsh worked as a logger and ranch hand, occupations as hard and dangerous as his avocation.

Blessed with artistic ability, he carved wooden figures and dabbled at sculpting but didn't pursue either. An interest in antique collectable bits and spurs provided the vehicle to focus his native ability. Admiring the old masters' work, Ernie was inspired to try bit and spur making. To learn the basics, he enrolled in the Miller Bit and Spur School located in Idaho, alma mater of many of today's leading artisans.

Enumclaw, Washington, was not exactly a hotbed of fine cowboy gear making. BMWs and Volvos were beginning to outnumber log trucks and pickup trucks on its streets. Seeking the companionship of like spirits, Ernie and wife Teresa found a refuge in John Day, a real buckaroo town, home to several western artisans. Association with them was a catalyst that stimulated Ernie's technical mastery and artistic genius.

Drawing on his extensive knowledge of historic bits and spurs, Ernie reworked traditional

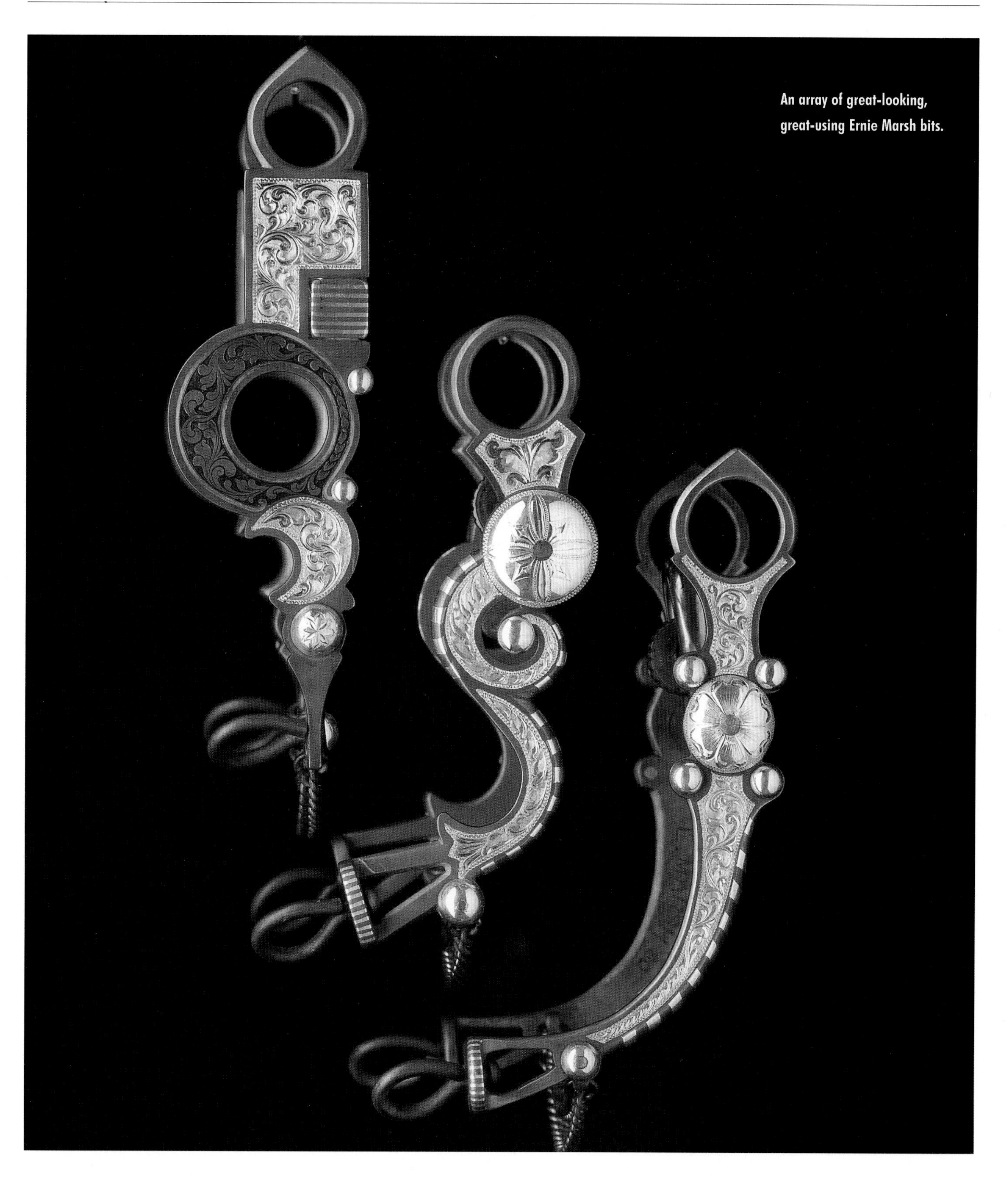

An array of great-looking, great-using Ernie Marsh bits.

styles and patterns. Teresa was a full partner, sharing the design and finishing work. Getting started wasn't easy. They ate a lot of bologna sandwiches and slept in the back of the pickup while traveling to bit and spur shows and western festivals. To them, these weren't hardships but challenges, because they loved what they were doing and were totally committed to it.

Marsh bits and spurs rapidly gained a following with working cowboys who valued the workmanship and utility of their gear. In a practice he still follows, Ernie consults with his clients, incorporating their insight into the bits and spurs he builds. Underlying function, even in his fanciest collector pieces, remains a passion. Ernie observes that "No matter how pretty a pair of spurs are, if they hurt your feet, they'll end up at home or in the pickup."

Searching for avenues to improve his finishing and decorative skills, Marsh enrolled in a gun-engraving school at Susanville, California. It was an artistic awakening, revealing new horizons of expression. In his hands, blank steel becomes a canvas. Engraving tools are like paintbrushes, allowing him to carve steel with precision, subtlety and flair, giving life and spirit to the cold, hard metal. Coupled with the soft French gray finish Ernie prefers, the engraving provides a perfect counterpoint to the finely worked silver adorning his bits and spurs. Things of beauty, each component complements the others to achieve a harmonized masterwork.

Marsh's artistry is matched by a fierce commitment to flawless construction. In addition to high-quality steels, Ernie uses advanced technological soldering techniques. He believes soldering creates a stronger, cleaner bond requiring less grinding and buffing to finish the piece. Outside the rodeo arena, the inglorious major cause of broken spurs is having them stepped on while leading a horse. In his years in the trade, this misfortune has yet to befall a pair of Ernie's spurs.

While enjoying making spurs, Marsh loves building bits, with their greater technical demands and requirement for "horse sense." Spades are a particular favorite. Ernie takes greater pride in compliments about how well a horse works with one of his bits than how pretty it is. In his words, "Things are functional first; the pretty comes later."

Ernie is flattered when working cowboys buy his gear. Their choice affirms that he is "making the gear right." Asked to name noted customers, without hesitation Marsh cited the cow boss of the Roaring Springs Ranch at French Glen, Oregon. Despite the flattery, Ernie is realist enough to know that a person would starve to death selling exclusively to working cowboys. To make a living, contemporary makers must market their gear to part-time hands and collectors, where Marsh has a large and growing following.

While a student of the old masters, Ernie believes contemporary makers are every bit as good, if not better. He feels such craftsmen as Mark Dahl don't have to pull their horns in for anybody. Beyond better tools, higher-grade metals and advanced metallurgy techniques, Marsh attributes the craft's remarkable renaissance to the cross-pollinating interaction between its artisans. Shared tips, ideas and healthy competition fosters constant innovative fomentation and a quest for excellence.

With the camaraderie that marks their guild, Ernie now helps aspiring young bit and spur makers with the same open, sharing spirit he was shown. He is mentoring his brother Jesse, a gifted artisan with a special talent for forging one-piece spurs, and emerging maker Greg Jones of Elgin, Oregon. Marsh is quick to acknowledge the contribution of Teresa, who shares all aspects of the work, particularly designing. Respected by his peers and revered by working cowboys and collectors, Marsh has earned a well-deserved reputation. He modestly defers any comparison to old-time makers as he savors his hard-won success. Ernie does concede he is a lucky man, doing the work he loves surrounded by the ones he loves. For now, that is more than enough.

MARK DAHL

On his ranch located between Deeth and Wells, Nevada, the very heartland of buckaroo country, Mark Dahl creates some of the finest traditional California-style bits and spurs being made today. Objects of exceptional beauty, they are prized by both collectors and working cowboys.

Like many leading contemporary craftsmen, ranch-raised Dahl is the product of a western upbringing. Cowboying came as second nature, while rodeoing was his hobby. Always enterprising, he did more than compete at rodeos. With his ready sense of humor, Dahl turned to rodeo clowning, developing an act featuring a pet steer he broke to ride. While he enjoyed the life, Mark knew it wouldn't provide a steady-enough income to keep food on the table and raise a family. Settling down, he returned to ranch life.

Ranching, however, has grown to be almost as big a gamble as rodeoing. It is a business at the mercy of fluctuating prices, drought, storm, disease and changing government regulations. Falling to the odds, many small ranchers have been forced from the range. For Dahl, bit and spur making has proven to be an insurance policy, evening the odds and protecting him from the vagaries besetting his neighbors.

Mark grew up being handy, a necessity of life on small family outfits. Able to weld, he repaired cowboy gear and eventually tried his hand at simple using equipment. Dahl discovered he had a flair for the work and enjoyed it. Being raised in the heart of buckaroo land, appreciation of fine gear was a birthright. He studied its use and construction firsthand every day. As his interest in

World Champion Bareback Rider Clint Corey proudly displays his three pairs of Mark Dahl spurs won at the Reno Rodeo.

Prime examples of Mark Dahl's acclaimed Mission-style bits. (Bits and headstalls courtesy of Vicky Mullins, Hitching Post Supply)

the craft grew, Dahl began to expand his artistic horizons, experimenting with silver engraving and application. Working with precious metals was a subject he knew absolutely nothing about. Largely self-taught, Mark had the advantage of studying the work of old-time masters such as those who had worked for the famed G. S. Garcia shop, just down the road in Elko.

By word of mouth, his reputation among local cowhands grew with his skills. With time, a transformation occurred. Instead of a rancher who made bits and spurs, he found himself as a bit and spur maker who ranched. He single-handedly keeps a steady stream of bits, spurs and jewelry rolling out of his workshop. With six children to feed, clothe and put through college, he has to be prolific.

Dahl employs a style known as western bright-cut engraving. He hand scribes a pattern of lines and cuts into the silver, creating intricate, light-reflecting designs, adding an extra dimension of beauty to his bits and spurs.

Dahl is particularly known for his exceptional interpretations of mission-style bits. He enjoys crafting these traditional pieces. In his hands, they are timeless. No two are exactly alike, so it is a fresh challenge every time he steps to the forge or sits at the workbench. His Santa Barbara, Las Cruces and Santa Paula bits are particularly prized. More than pretty showpieces, they are meticulously constructed—particularly the spade mouthpieces—and balanced, making them great using bits.

In an interesting marketing experiment for fine custom gear, Dahl has collaborated with the owners of Hitching Post Supply, who commissioned a series of mission-style bits.

As a Nevada native, Dahl is practically obliged to make fancy, eye-catching grapplin' irons. Working in the California style, he features richly engraved inlaid silver, elaborately forged heel bands and shanks, chap guards and jingle bobs. His buzz saws are a buckaroo's pride and joy. Complemented by a pair of finely tooled spur straps with Dahl's silver conchos and buckles, they are about as pretty a sight as a cowboy could imagine. No fancy playthings intended for the fireplace mantle or den wall, though; these are made for the rough and tumble atmosphere of ranch life. Dahl guarantees the silver will not come off his spurs, a guarantee he has not had to back up yet.

While collectors line up to buy his California drag rowels, Dahl's most famous spurs are not for sale. They can only be won in the crucible of the Reno Rodeo's arena. In a popular tradition, Mark makes spurs for the event winners. The Reno Rodeo has become associated with its championship spurs.

Without being boastful, Dahl believes there are higher-quality, prettier bits and spurs being made today than in the era of Garcia and Morales. He is intimately familiar with their work and appreciative of what they achieved with the tools and materials of their time. Mark acknowledges the advantages he and other leading contemporary makers enjoy. Succinctly put, Dahl says, "When the electricity goes off, I'm shut down." Technology aside, aficionados of the craft staunchly maintain that Dahl's work belongs at the top in any era.

Like many other leading artisans, Dahl is extremely thankful for the cowboy revival movement and the attention it has brought to his bits and spurs. With a clientele reaching far beyond the cowboy's traditional range, he can earn a living doing something he enjoys while being where he wants to be. Thanks to his craft, he can raise his children in a traditional ranch setting and pass on the beliefs and lifestyle he cherishes. Not too bad for someone who started out as a clown.

Mark Dahl's exceptional silverwork distinguishes his bits and spurs. (Bit courtesy of Vicky Mullins, Hitching Post Supply)

Starkly modern and cutting edge, Tom Balding's welds decorate his articulated bit.

TOM BALDING

Tom Balding is living proof that western gear making is not a closed shop. No one has ridden a more crooked trail to the top of the trade than Tom. A Southern California native and archetypical beachboy, he grew up in a surfing and sailing culture. His youthful battle cries were "surfs up" and "hang ten," not "cowboy up" or "let 'er buck."

His jobs were a young Californian's dream, working as a welder for Holly Header's racing program and Hobie Cat sailboats. Welding was a passion, a calling. He rapidly became an expert. Between fast cars and sailing, it was an endless summer existence.

Sought after for precision jobs, Balding opened a custom welding business catering to the aerospace and high-performance sailboat industries. Riding his welding mastery, the company flourished. Despite commercial success, living in Southern California was increasingly unrewarding.

Making a dramatic change, Tom sold the business and forsook California's beach culture for Wyoming's high-plains cowboy lifestyle. Beyond questioning his sanity, Balding's amazed friends asked how he planned to earn a living in Wyoming's alien environment. In honesty, Tom didn't know. What he did know was, no matter what it took, he would find a way.

Balding set out for Sheridan, Wyoming. The destination was not selected by whim. Sheridan represented the reawakening of a childhood dream. Tom shared a love of the cowboy West with his father. His family vacationed in its wide-open spaces, adventurously following where back roads led. Sheridan was one of those places. Tom never forgot the town and its surrounding country.

Determined to make a place for himself, Balding took entry-level jobs. He built miles of fence and bucked tons of hay. Barely scraping by, Tom contemplated taking up saddle making. A chance encounter, however, rendered the option irrelevant. A local woman brought him a broken bit to repair. After inspecting it, Tom asked if she wanted one that would never break. Although opting for a repair job, she sparked a lightning streak of inspiration. With a burst of clarity, he saw his place in Sheridan's cowboy culture. That night Balding built a bit. After the inspiration came the perspiration. Months went into building prototype spurs, bits and the jigs to make

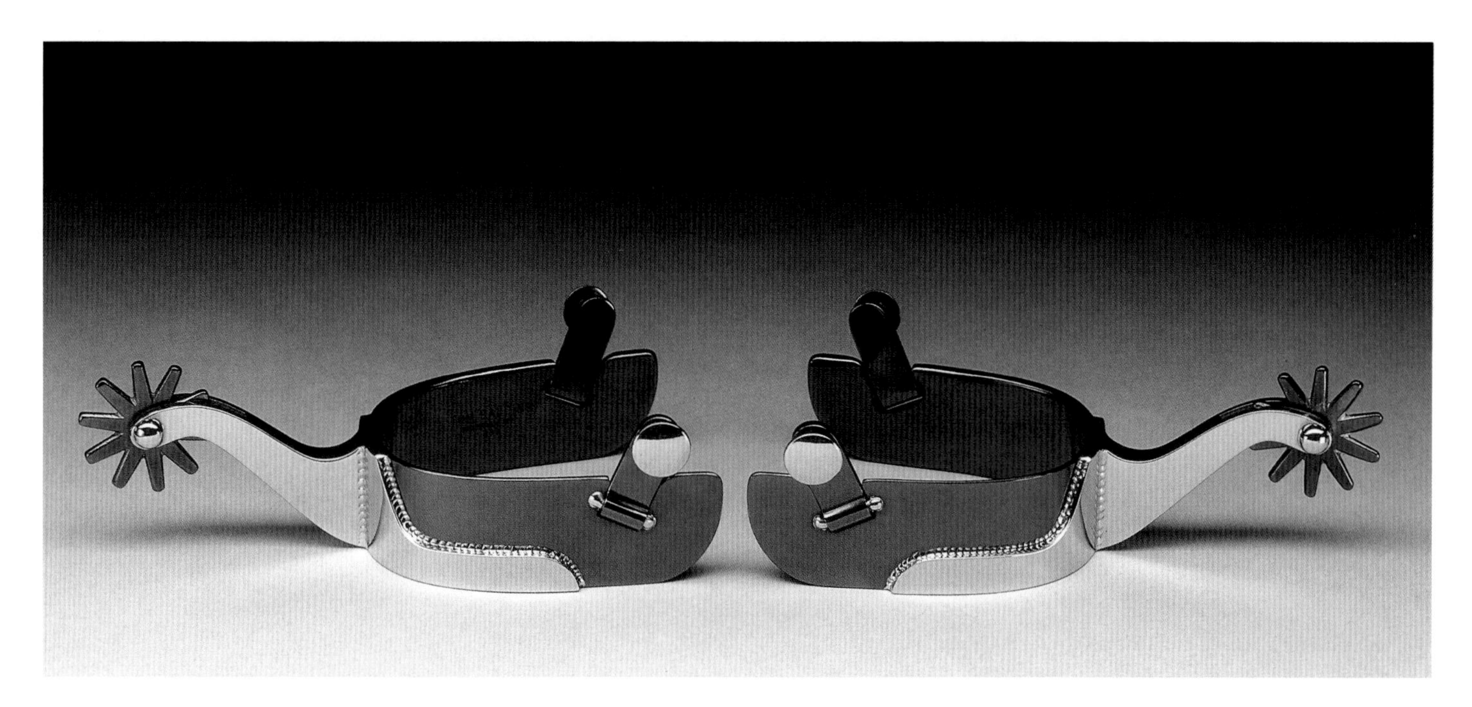

A pair of Tom Balding's flawlessly finished spurs.

them. A year later, he was ready for production.

The bits employed concepts borrowed from sailing technology, utilized advanced metallurgy techniques, and featured his peerless welding skills. His revolutionary bits are articulated, combining the flexible action of a snaffle with the leverage of a port. With precision ball bearings and flawless finishing, the bits do not bind. Advanced ultrasonic equipment removes any construction debris that might foul moving parts or mar the finish.

With prototypes in hand, Tom solicited the opinion of Don Butler, a leading Sheridan saddle maker and owner of the Cowboy Custom Shop. Impressed, Butler recommended Balding take his wares to a reining show in Gillette. Down and nearly out, Tom gambled and made the trip. The gamble paid off. He took two dozen orders for bits and spurs and has been behind ever since.

Tom makes primarily snaffles and grazing-type bits. His audience is working and rodeo cowboys, trainers, and cutting and reining horse people. While Tom claims not to be a silversmith and focuses on function, he creates objects of stark, modernistic beauty. A maestro with welding tools, his welds are integral to the object's decoration. While other artisans grind and buff away evidence of their welds, Balding's beads are laid down with precision and artistic flair, becoming part of the design. Balding's finish—a product of hours of meticulous buffing and polishing—has mirrorlike brilliance and depth.

Tom continues to develop new bit designs. Currently his repertoire includes approximately two hundred models. Balding views his trade as never perfected, offering the continual challenge of making better bits and spurs. If imitation is the sincerest form of flattery, Balding is among the West's most flattered men.

Now a fixture in Sheridan, Tom has opened a store in town to sell his bits and spurs. He has come a long way since he pulled into town searching for a new beginning. He consorts with many of the leading lights in cutting, reining and showing. Three-time World Reining Champion Bobby Ingersoll, acclaimed horseman Buck Brannaman, leading reining-trainer Bob Loomis, top cutting-horse man Dick Pieper, many-time NFR pickup man Kenny Clabaugh, and Rodeo Hall of Fame Saddle Bronc Rider Clint Johnson all swear by Balding's gear. Tom Balding has indeed found his home.

A COWBOY'S HISTORY OF HITCHING & BRAIDING

Since ancient times, man has twisted, braided and woven animal and plant fibers to serve his needs. They have formed the fabric of life. From Egypt's pyramids to Anasazi cliff dwellings, anthropologists measure the sophistication of long-vanished peoples by fiber fragments.

Like our ancient ancestors, cowboys remain in contact with the natural world, its rhythms dictating the pace of their days. In common bond, the cowboy's tools still come directly from nature, linking them to the long ago with unbroken cords of hide and hair.

His hat is of fur felt or straw, his boots of hide. He sits a saddle of leather and wood, joining man and horse in reaffirmation of their ancient partnership. Headstalls, reins, bosals, hobbles, quirts, hackamores and "McCartys"—tools of hide and hair—remain staples of the cowboy trade.

The ancient crafts of plaiting rawhide and horsehair have been elevated to a true native art form by the Mexican vaquero and American cowboy. Braiding and knot tying remain basic cowboy skills, essential to making gear and expedient repairs. They are also social conventions. Get a few hands together and pretty soon someone is making up a halter, putting a hondo in a lariat or braiding a bronc rein out of bailing twine.

Before long, one of the boys will ask to have a new knot demonstrated. In no time, a braiding bee is underway. While the average cowboy's work is usually pretty rough, the nimble fingers and calculating mind of the gifted braider or hitcher endow their creations with functional beauty.

Hitching and braiding are closely related crafts. Many artisans are adept at both, often incorporating both techniques in the same piece. Over time, however, the crafts have come to differ in purpose. While rawhide gear remains close to its hardscrabble working origins, most contemporary horsehair hitching is decorative, intended for the showring or den wall rather than the range. Both crafts, however, are in the midst of a dazzling revival. Gifted artisans are producing gear of exceptional quality, originality and beauty. Unlike old-time saddle, bit and spur makers, most hitchers and braiders of vintage gear are nameless. It is important, therefore, that today's artisans leave their mark and not be relegated to the obscurity of their predecessors. The profiled craftsmen, representative of the many excellent hitchers and braiders practicing these classic cowboy art forms, give a human face to these time-honored crafts.

A pair of cuffs by Casey Backus featuring horsehair hitching, rawhide braiding and leather tooling. (Cuffs courtesy of the author)

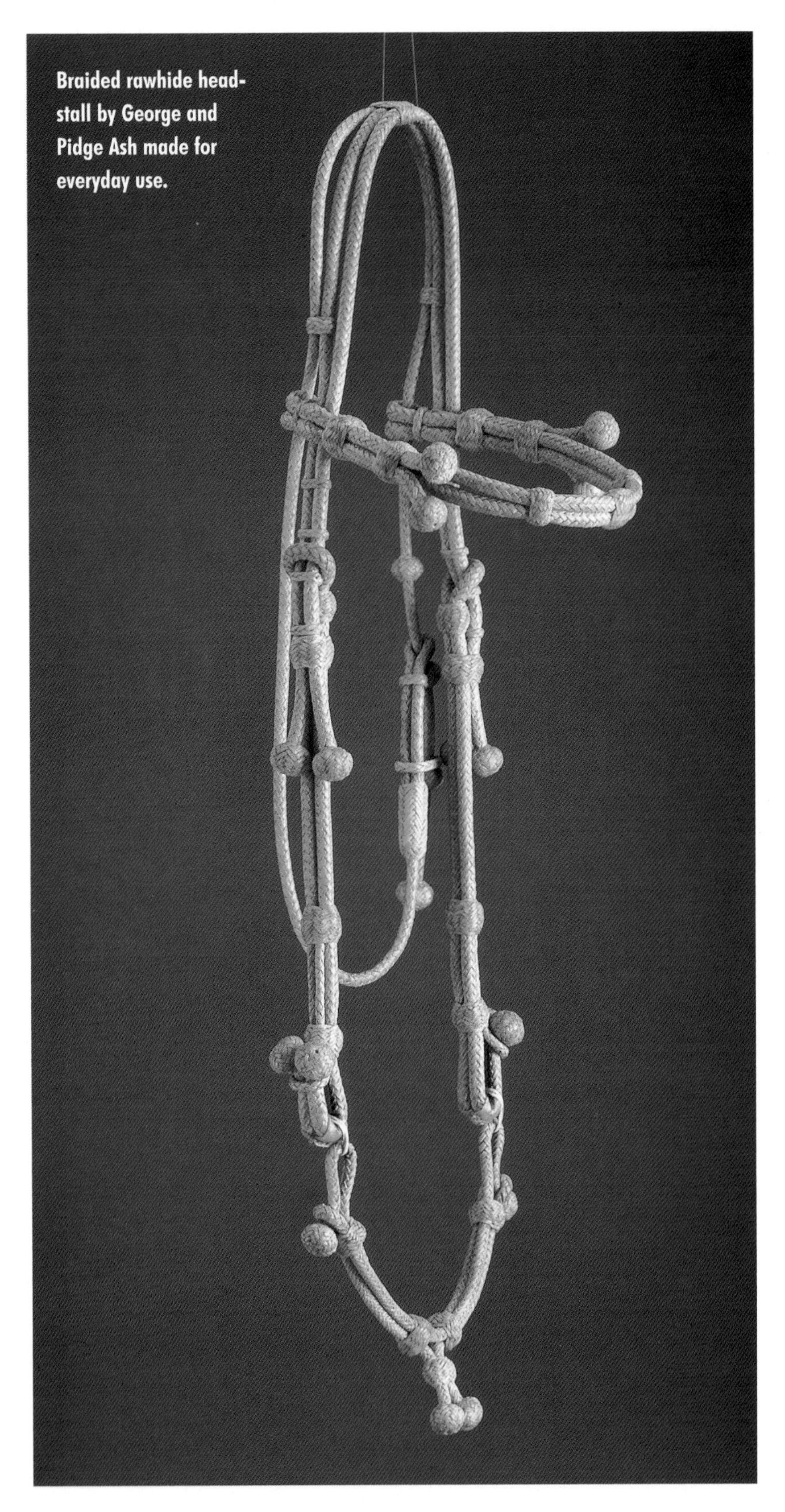

Braided rawhide headstall by George and Pidge Ash made for everyday use.

BRAIDING

Today's rawhiders practice a skill stretching across history. It remains a very human endeavor; no machine can replace the artisan. With seasoned eye and practiced hand, he cuts long rawhide thongs, widening or narrowing the width to accommodate the hide's thickness, ensuring uniform size and strength. Sophisticated robotics can't plait eight of these thongs for half their length and then double them back, skillfully interweaving the cords through the original braiding to produce sixteen strands. When practiced by a master, western historian J. Frank Dobie maintained that western rawhide braiding "for texture, symmetry, flexibility, balance of weight and gradation of diameter equals in workmanship the accomplishment of any weaving, whether of basket or blanket, of any time."

Braided rawhide horse gear reached a peak in vaquero California. *Reateros* and *trenzadors* were revered for their skills. These braiders were also good hands who savvied how their rawhide tack was used. From the days of the Dons, families have nurtured and perpetuated the craft, passing it from generation to generation. The Ortegas are the most revered rawhiding clan. Recently deceased, Louis Ortega upheld the family tradition. Perhaps the greatest rawhider to practice the trade, the fineness and uniformity of his rawhide strands and intricacy of his knots set enduring standards of excellence.

Like so much in life, successful braiding begins with careful preparation and good materials. Most leading braiders "fix" their own hides. The fixing process appears to be the epitome of simplicity. Rawhide essentially makes itself, for nature does most of the work. As with most simple things, however, many complex truths lie behind the making of a quality hide.

A rawhide's life begins with the demise of its original owner. There is considerable debate regarding which animals produce the best hides. Some favor thin or sick animals while others favor particular breeds, such as the Black Angus.

For some purposes, the hide of a big, old bull is held to be the only thing. In all cases, the sooner the animal is skinned after shaking off its mortal coil, the better. Care in skinning is essential. When removed, it is called a "green hide." If dried without treatment, it is a "flint hide."

The green hide is staked out in the shade and dried until stiff. After scraping the flesh side, the rawhider cuts a circle from the center of the hide. Like peeling an apple in a continuous spiral, the artisan cuts the circle of hide into a two- to three-inch-wide strip. Done properly, the strip will have uniform width and, more importantly, strength when dried.

The rawhider continues the strip's preparation by cutting off or "slipping" the hair through chemical action. Soaking the hide in running water for four to five days is the simplest method. The chemical concoctions in the slip and slack process are classically vernacular. The mixtures range from a "milk" of lime and water slacked by a lactic acid bath to pastes of ash, preferably from hardwoods, to the lethal-sounding lime and red arsenic. Additionally, the rawhider can use a variety of salting techniques. Each process has champions who claim their hides have greater firmness, life, body and strength.

When ready, the rawhide is cut into strings. The finer the intended work, the narrower the strings. Often, the cut is beveled to ensure a smooth, tight-fitting braid. A variety of devices are used to cut the strings. Simplest is freehanding with a sharp knife and calloused thumb. Improvised machines range from a bent nail securing a blade to a piece of wood to elaborate contraptions with adjustable blade settings and pulleys to feed the strip to the cutting surface.

Before braiding can begin, the strings must

Casey Backus braided stock whip with a turned black-walnut handle.

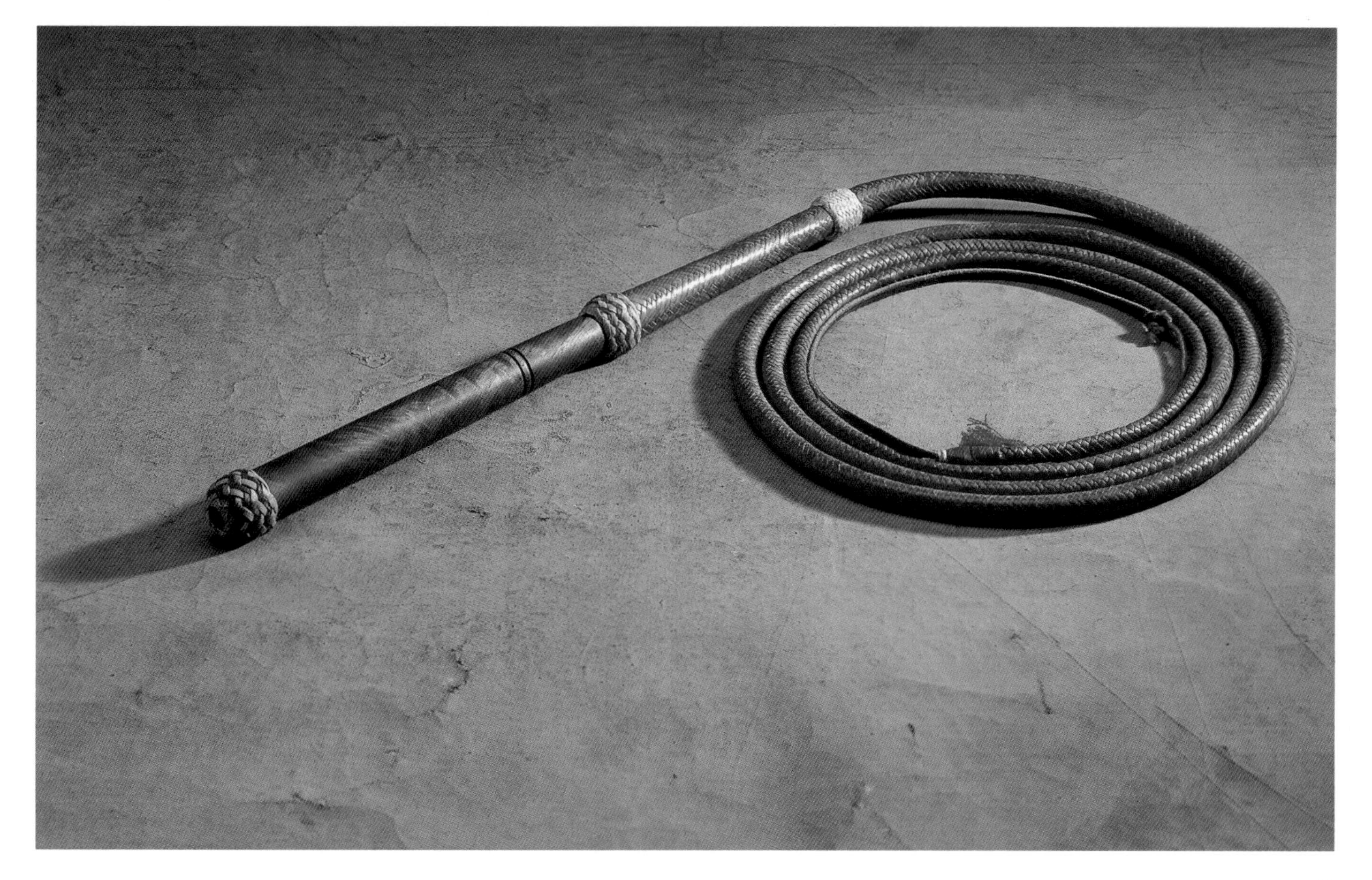

be conditioned. This softens the strings and provides uniform consistency and diameter. Tempered with saddle soap or neat's-foot oil, the rawhider works out hard spots and shapes the strings, employing the concept of making a square peg fit a round hole. This includes pulling the string through a slotted piece of wood or drawing it through progressively smaller holes drilled in a board. Having completed this trial by torture, the strings are ready to be "braided up" into a piece of working gear.

Many of the rawhider's tools would be familiar to his ancient kin crouched outside the cave. While today's rawhider uses a knife of steel instead of flint, the other tools haven't changed much since men went courting with a club. Fids—gougelike instruments with thin, rounded points—are often made from a sheep's bone. Other primal tools include gauges—pieces of bone or wood with holes of different diameters—and mandrels—sticks with four facets and a rawhide or leather collar used to braid knots.

With strings and tools in hand, the braider is ready to transform the spaghetti-like rawhide strands into a piece of horse gear. To top braiders, the process is a symbiotic relationship between the mathematical precision of braiding formulas expressed in parts and bights (the greater the number of parts and bights the more complex the braid) and a genius for design, which elevates their work to functional art. For master rawhiders, the process is much like writing music. The relationship between bights and the number of strings provides structure to the creative process, just as notes and chords are the composer's building blocks.

By varying patterns and injecting color via dyed strings, the artisan imparts visual drama to his creation. Finely braided knots or buttons punctuate the piece with bold highlights. Colorfully named knots—Spanish Rings, Turk's Heads, Pineapples and Sheep's Heads—are intricate puzzles. They give shape and form, purpose and function to the flaccid strands of hide. More than decoration, the knots and buttons fasten, adjust and weight the gear, directly contributing to its utility.

Many westerners feared fine rawhide work faced extinction in the 1960s and '70s. The increased value of time, mass production, offshore manufacturing and synthetic materials threatened to price rawhide gear out of the marketplace. Additionally, some old-timers refused to pass on trade secrets, carrying them to the grave rather than passing knowledge to a new generation of rawhiders. Not only has rawhiding confounded the prophets of doom by surviving, it has flourished. The skilled fingers and inventive minds of today's masters are taking the craft to new heights from which they can see not only the long back trail of rawhiding's history but the gleaming vistas of a bright tomorrow.

Hitching

While the finest rawhide braiding of the West's classical era occurred among the vaqueros of old California, horsehair hitching reached its zenith on the northern plains within the past century. To survive, rawhide braiding has stuck with its working origins. Hitching, however, has expanded its artistic potential to pay the freight in the late twentieth century. Although functional, hitched-hair gear is far more delicate than comparable rawhide articles. Strikingly attractive, hitched gear is eagerly sought by avid collectors and showring competitors anxious to complement beautiful mounts with the finest of tack.

The genesis of western hair work lies with Europe and the cowboys of the northern plains. The Victorian handicraft of making human-hair ornaments shares the family tree. Manifestations of a maudlin era, Victorians fashioned locks of a loved one's hair into "jewelry of sentiment." Made from a baby's curls, the tresses of a daughter bound for Oregon or a deathbed lock of a loved one bound for the Great Beyond, they were tangible links to cherished times and kin.

An eye-dazzling display of Alfredo Campos reins and quirts.

The intricate, complex and time-consuming process of hitching.

Instructional manuals for creating human-hair ornaments were widely available. For less sentimental, more practical cowboys, it was an easy step to transfer the techniques from human to horse hair, producing decorative tools rather than keepsakes. For men with clever hands and long Montana or Wyoming winter nights to fill, hitching was a natural diversion. A true bunkhouse pastime, cowboys "knotted up" colorful headstalls, reins and quirts, putting a little flash in their rigs.

A handicraft in the bunkhouse, hitching was

elevated to an art form in the "big house." Hitching hair requires time and distraction-free concentration, commodities incarceration provided in spades. In prisons at Lame Deer, Laramie, and Walla Walla, cowboys who were too handy with the rope and careless with the branding iron passed their time as guests of the state hitching horsehair items. "Makin' hair bridles" became the vernacular for doing jail time. Discussing an acquaintance, Charlie Russell wrote:

> Charley Cugar quit punchin' and went into the cow business for himself. His start was a couple o' cows and a work bull. Each cow had six to eight calves a year. People didn't say much till the bull got to havin' calves, and then they made it so disagreeable that Charley quit the business and is now makin' hoss-hair bridles.

Of the four types of western hair work—hitching, braiding, weaving and twisting—hitching is the highest art form. Difficult to learn, demanding to master and infinitely time consuming, hitching consists of tying bundles of horsehair, or pulls, in series after series of tiny knots around a trellislike string core.

Horse mane and tail hair is hitching's basic ingredient. Mane hair, being finer, is preferred for intricate work. After the hair is pulled from the horse, it is detangled, washed, dried and dyed. The prepared hairs are twisted together, forming threadlike strands called "pulls" or "strings." The hair's thickness and the intricacy of a project determine how many hairs are twisted into the pull. While there is no standard, generally ten to twelve hairs go into a pull for average projects, while as few as six or seven form the pull for a really fine piece of hitching.

The finer and more consistent the knots, the better the hitching. Colored hair and patterned knots produce designs. The nature of the process lends itself to geometric patterns and spirals. Within the medium's confines, it is possible to create representational figures; flags, letters, numerals and stylized animals.

Hitching is not a static craft, bound to endless repetition of time-honored designs. Innovative hitchers such as Colorado's Alex Papas and Doug Krouse are pioneering new techniques, expanding and energizing the craft. By easing extra strands into the pull and adjusting the knot spacing, they are able to create smoother, more natural-looking figures like hearts, flowers, birds and buffaloes.

Producing masterpieces, however, requires more than time and craftsmanship. Impeccable vision, a symbiotic blend of mechanics and artistry, is essential to becoming a topflight hitcher. Employing color and pattern, today's best hitchers create tapestry-like pieces of great complexity and sophistication. In so doing, they are elevating the craft to a higher plateau of artistry. Collectively, they are invigorating a craft that a generation ago appeared moribund. For future generations, these hitched masterpieces will have captured in rich colors and subtle textures the spirit of the West.

HITCHERS AND BRAIDERS

Hitched bosal with braided rawhide noseband fashioned by Casey Backus.

CASEY BACKUS

Cheyenne. The name rolls off the tongue with an easy western gait. Immortalized in song and verse, and home of the "Daddy of 'Em All" Frontier Days Rodeo, it is still true to its cowboy roots. The modern stock saddle was perfected in shops along its dusty cow-town streets. Cattle barons toasted success in the opulent Cheyenne Social Club. With its rich western heritage, it is fitting that talented hitcher and braider Casey Backus calls Cheyenne home.

Casey was lured to Cheyenne's bright lights from his native Chugwater, Wyoming. Chugwater is as "ranchy" as a town can get. It was once headquarters of the legendary Swan Land and Cattle Company. If you're from Chugwater, you're western. Backus grew up on the family ranch breaking colts, working cattle and riding bucking horses for fun. He earned a rodeo scholarship to the University of Wyoming and competed in the PRCA.

During college he dabbled at leather working and braiding, eventually landing a job with noted Cheyenne saddler Tony Holmes. Also working in the shop was another youngster, Doug Krause. The two shared a mutual interest in hitching. Casey wanted a hitched hatband, so they decided to make one.

Krause knew how to twist hair into pulls but little more. In search of knowledge, they headed to the Cheyenne Public Library. All they found was a pamphlet published in 1920, which the librarian allowed them to copy. Armed with its scant guidance, they started hitching, employing ingenuity to fill gaps in the text. Critiquing each other's work, they learned by doing and developed unique styles unfettered by rote repetition of traditional techniques and patterns. Although it was the hard way, it was worth the effort, for both developed into leading hitchers.

Even with today's improved instructional materials, hitching remains a challenging craft to master. Backus maintains that a basic requirement is "the heart to stick with it till you get it figured out." Mastering the mechanics, however, doesn't guarantee a top hitcher. Artistry can't be taught. Casey is gifted with a flair for design and color coordination that elevates his work beyond the ordinary. Coupled with his ambition to expand the craft's horizons with unique, out-of-the-ordinary pieces, Backus has become a force in contemporary hitching.

Unique to Casey's work is the integration of leather tooling, rawhide and leather braiding, and horsehair hitching into multidiscipline masterpieces. Being self-taught, his designs reflect a unique individualism. Representational figures such as birds, flowers, buffaloes and arrows increasingly distinguish his work.

Backus enjoys the challenge of matching the artistry of conception with the mechanics of construction. He likens himself to a painter doing "studies" as he prepares for major projects. He spends hours hitching prototypes until he achieves the pattern he wants.

Casey adamantly believes that high-quality hair is essential to excellent hitching. For special projects and commissions, Backus pulls and prepares the hair himself. Not only does this assure uniformity and quality control, the hair of a favorite horse adds extra significance to commissioned pieces. Currently, Backus gets his commercial hair from companies in Pennsylvania and New York whose regular customers use the hair for brushes and violin bows.

If Backus had his way, he would make nothing but bosals, headstalls, quirts and reins. As a working cowboy, he appreciates seeing the fruits of his labors used, not consigned to collectors' walls.

Backus attends few shows because it takes so much time to create special pieces highlighting his hitching, braiding and leather work. Hitching aficionados, including Roger Allgeier of Brighton Feed and Farm Supply in Brighton, Colorado, feature Casey's work in their collections. Working cowboys in Colorado, Wyoming and Montana put his rawhide gear to the test every day. Noted rodeo cowboys such as NFR bull rider Mark Cain and top PRCA bull fighter Rick Chatman sport his creations. Backus and his hitching have come a long way from his after-hours struggles at Tony Holmes' saddle shop. When the Queen of Jordan is a client, your fame has spread far beyond Chugwater.

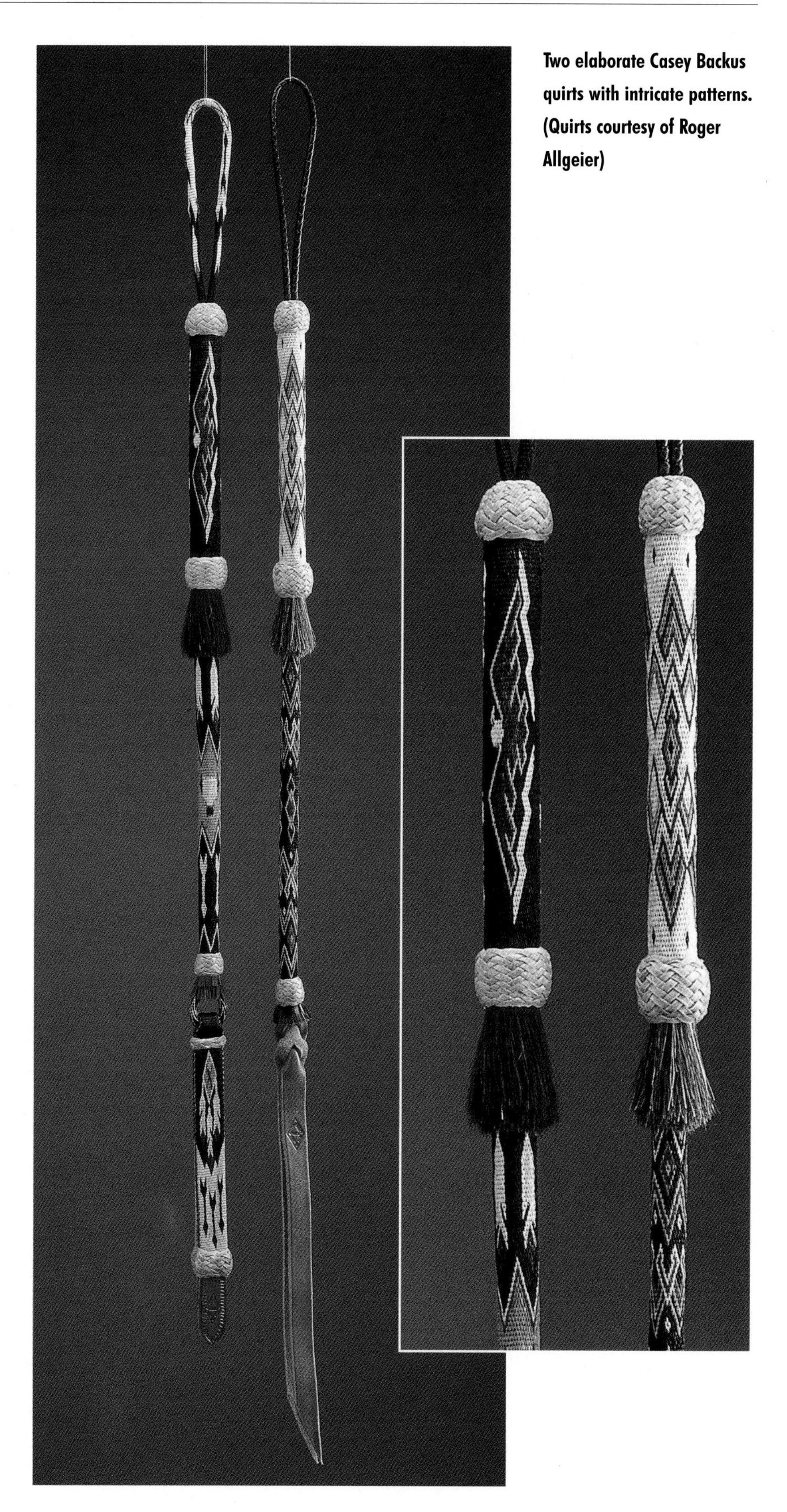

Two elaborate Casey Backus quirts with intricate patterns. (Quirts courtesy of Roger Allgeier)

A colorful mosaic of Alfredo Campos hitching.

Alfredo Campos

Braiding was a Campos family tradition practiced for generations. As a young man on his family's ranch near Tucson, Arizona, Alfredo created rawhide reatas and horse gear. He was captivated by the process of turning raw hides into beautiful tools.

Reatas, the vaquero's traditional braided rawhide rope, were his passion, but the age of reatas was rapidly passing. So, too, was the age of the small, multigenerational family ranch. Victim of economic change, Alfredo abandoned the vaquero life of his ancestors to seek a living where he could find it. The search took him far from the sunny Sonoran desert to Boeing Aircraft in the Pacific Northwest's cool, gray clime.

He poured the craftsman's pride that distinguished his reatas into Boeing's aircraft. Recognizing Alfredo's creative powers, Boeing plucked him from the assembly line and assigned him to a team creating specialized tools and jigs to fabricate the giant planes.

By day, he built jets. By night, he braided rawhide, its cords linking him to his lost vaquero life. In his economic exile, Alfredo became aware of hitching, a skill little practiced in the Southwest. In the age before instructional videos and self-help craft manuals, Alfredo was left to his own devices in mastering the complex art form. With a few historic prison pieces to study, a facile mind and hours of trial and error, Alfredo taught himself to hitch.

Hitching has an underlying arithmetic logic. Once grasped, it is a matter of dividends and divisors that translate into patterns and colors. Campos, however, hitches hair like a composer, not an engineer. Like a symphonic composition, his calculations create works alive with color and movement, a complementary whole formed from precisely patterned knots. Other hitchers marvel at Alfredo's ability to pattern even the most complex knots, such as the cap topping a quirt. It is an ability that sets him apart from his contemporaries, marking him as one of the world's leading hitchers.

A traditionalist to the core, Campos originally hitched only natural-color hair, believing it to be authentic, but viewing a rainbow-hued collection of vintage prison hitching disabused him of this notion. With his palette unhobbled, Alfredo embraced color with enthusiasm, hitching with a kaleidoscopic profusion of bold hues.

While Alfredo approaches his palette with gusto, his knots, the actual mechanical process of hitching, are executed with machinelike precision. Perfectly aligned, closely spaced and smooth, they are criterions of exceptional craftsmanship. Alfredo's quality-control standards are like Boeing's—zero defects. Even on close examination, you will not find a gap, a missed hitch or misaligned knot. It is not uncommon for Campos to rip out hours of painstaking work to correct a minor flaw that would escape all but his eye.

Modestly, Campos attributes his masterpieces to doing the math, meticulous attention

Known primarily for his spectacular hitching, Alfredo Campos is also an adept hand with a reata.

to selecting and preparing the hair, and spending the time to hitch as tightly and evenly as possible. Time is a critical element, one that not everyone can afford. Now retired, Alfredo can concentrate on his hitching, free from the tyranny of production schedules and deadlines. Having raised a family, he appreciates the challenge facing hitchers with young families and house payments. The challenge limits the number of people who stick with the craft long enough to truly master its intricacies. The process is so time consuming that even the most acclaimed hitchers with avid followings among well-heeled collectors don't make much when they figure out their pay by the hour.

Volume isn't an objective with Alfredo. Consequently, his work is always in demand. Most of his projects are special orders and he maintains a steady backlog. Like most hitchers who were working cowboys, his favorite projects are horse trappings: headstalls, reins, bosals and quirts. To a traditionalist who loves beautiful tools, they represent the ultimate expression of the hitcher's art.

Dyed rawhide strings add visual drama to quirts and reins with romel by the Ash family.

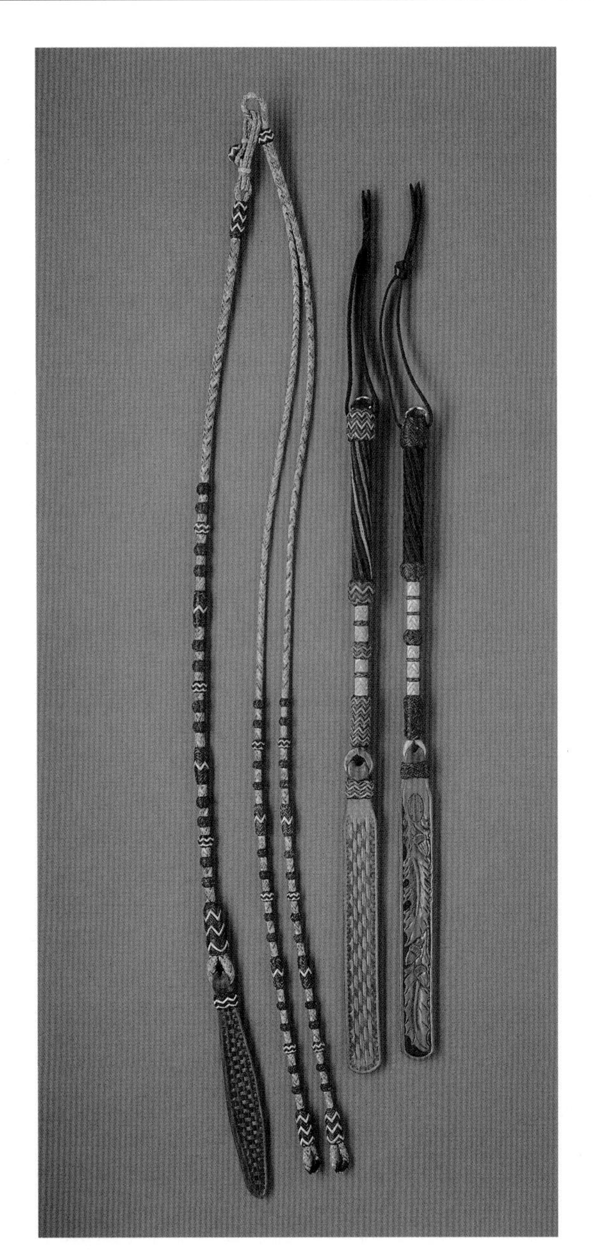

The Ash Family

Braiding is the tie that binds for the Ash family of Kooskia, Idaho. Rawhide strings are common threads in this close-knit family comprised of George and Pidge Ash, their sons Harv and Ben and daughter Chris Hunter.

Kooskia is typical of small western towns struggling to weather changing economic conditions and federal regulations. The local economy depends on cattle and timber. Currently, cattle prices are falling but trees aren't, causing ranches and sawmills to go under. For the Ashes, braiding rawhide horse gear provides an alternative to moving to the city in search of work. The traditional western craft allows them to live a traditional western life.

They came to the trade naturally. Pidge's family were noted rawhiders. When George married into the clan, part of the dowry was an education in braiding rawhide.

Initially, George braided rawhide and built saddles on the side while working a variety of cowboying, logging and sawmill jobs to provide for a growing family. Even at this early stage, his work developed a reputation for quality among local cowboys.

With their children grown, George and Pidge channeled much of their newfound time into braiding and leather work. Luckily, George was an able teacher and Pidge an adept pupil. While the family that braids together may stay together, it is not a craft that stimulates conversation. Although they work in the same room, George and Pidge focus on their braiding projects with such intensity that talking is a distraction.

They make all types of rawhide horse tack from plain working gear to fancy special orders. Their basic gear is made with the same attention to detail and quality materials as the flashier showpiece headstalls, reins, bosals and quirts. The Ashes find that producing a stock of standard items while mixing in custom orders is a sound economic practice.

While sharing all aspects of the business, Pidge leaves the larger-diameter pieces—anything above 5/8 inch, such as quirts, big bosals and large heel knots—to George, because it requires a great deal of strength to pull the strings through the complex maze of braids. The handicraft is hard on the hands. Occasionally, they have to take a few days off to let their hands rest.

When recuperating, however, they concentrate on other aspects of the process such as preparing hides. Rawhiders were recyclers long before the concept became popular. When neighbors butcher or a cow falls victim to the perils of the range, the Ashes get a call. Only the best hides, correctly processed, make it into their gear. Besides preparing the hides, George also cuts all the strings true and fine.

George adds color to their work by dyeing some of the strings. When worked into the braiding, their blacks, browns and reds create appealing herringbone patterns. Coupled with stylish knots and "buttons," their work is as attractive as it is functional. While their working gear makes sure the bills are paid, George and Pidge enjoy the custom orders emphasizing braiding's artistry. Employing color, elaborate knots, lavish use of buttons, leather work, hitching and horsehair tassels, they create works of envy. Still, they keep their projects usable, foregoing ultra fancy, tiny strings and knots that won't stand up to the rigors of ranch life.

Color and pattern add flair to a bosal by George and Pidge Ash.

While supporting and encouraging each other, the Ash siblings pursue their crafts independently, maintaining their own clients. Harv hitches and braids when he isn't logging. Ben, injured in a bronc-riding accident, makes custom boots as well as braiding. Chris is also multitalented. A trained wheelwright, she also makes exceptionally fine mohair and wool cinches.

Pidge says, "If you have to work, braiding isn't a bad way to make a living." Actually, retirement isn't a concept that appeals to the Ashes. Reflecting on their success in a rare quiet moment, Pidge modestly sums up their family as "a little outfit that things happened to work out right for."

Sources

Saddles

Monte Beckman
79 N. Main
Moab, UT 84532
(801) 259-3006

Scott Brown & Gray Dunshee
Big Bend Saddlery
P.O. Box 38
East Hwy 90
Alpine, TX 79831
(1-800) 634-4502, fax (915) 837-7278

Rich Boyer
Boyer Saddlery
201 E. Main
Hermiston, OR 97838
(503) 567-2536

Eddie Brooks
Elko, NV
(702) 738-8873

W. C. Hape
Custom Saddlery
1672 Warren Ave.
Sheridan, WY 82801
(307) 674-5270

Dusty Harvey
Lawrence Saddlery
28 S.W. Court
Pendleton, OR 97801
(541) 278-0818

Dale Harwood
Trails End Saddle Shop
Shelly, ID
(208) 357-3803

King Saddlery
Sheridan, WY 82801
(1-800) 443-8919, (307) 672-2702,
fax (307) 672-5235

Bob Klenda
Klenda Custom Made Saddles
6123 City Rd. 214
New Castle, CO 81647
(303) 984-2741

Ed Kline Saddlery
1619 U.S. Hwy. 50
Grand Junction, CO 81503
(303) 241-1881

Patrick Lee
Patrick's Saddlery
HCR 01, Box 95
Mt. Vernon, OR 97865
(541) 932-4532

Bob Marrs Saddle Shop
102 Rancho Trail
Amarillo, TX 79108
(806) 383-7711

Nancy Petersen
Three Forks Saddlery
221 S. Main
Three Forks, MT 59752
(406) 285-3459, fax (406) 285-3422

D. D. Potter
Potter Saddlery
3105 S.E. Court, Suite 4
Pendleton, OR 97801
(541) 276-0677

Wes Schenck
Schenck's Saddlery
37 N. Central
Harlowton, MT 59036
(406) 632-5893

Severe Brothers Saddlery
P.O. Box 1453
Pendleton, OR 97801
(541) 276-2961

Chuck Stormes
Stormes Saddle Company
210 3628 Burnsland Rd. S.E.
Calgary, Alberta, T2G 3Z2 Canada
(403) 287-9671

Ken Tipton
TIPS Western
185 Melarkey St.
Winnemucca, NV 89445
(1-800) 547-8477

Jeremiah Watt
Custom Saddlery
Van Dyke Ranch
HC1, Box 34
Coalinga, CA 93210
(209) 935-2172, fax (209) 935-1021

Bits and Spurs

Tom Balding Bits and Spurs
380 Mead Creek Rd.
Sheridan, WY 82801
(307) 672-8459

Bill Bear
Bear Enterprises
P.O. Box 1856
Bear Ranch Rd.
Elko, NV 89801
(702) 738-8534, fax (702) 738-9775

Robert and Leon Campbell
Campbell Bit and Spurs
6636 River Rd.
Amarillo, TX 79108
(806) 381-0873

Jerry Cates
Cates Bits and Spurs
5235 Slope
Amarillo, TX 79108
(806) 383-6030

Mark Dahl
Deeth, NV
(702) 752-3475

Lon Davis
High Noon Bit and Spur
P.O. Box 702
John Day, OR 97845
(503) 575-1101

Jerry Ginn
HC 66, Box 495
Kooskia, ID 83539-9609
(208) 926-7203

The Hayes Family
Bits of Silver
6905 Sycamore
Atascadero, CA 93422
(805) 461-3297

Bill Heisman
6550 N. Desert View Dr.
Tucson, AZ 85743
(602) 682-7537

Greg Jones
GKJ Bit and Spur
71316 Valley View Rd.
Elgin, OR 97827
(541) 437-0801

Jerry Kauffman
JBT Spurs
1674 Main St.
Longmont, CO 80601
(303) 772-2191

Ernie Marsh
Marsh Bit and Spur
HCR 56, Box 820
John Day, OR 97845
(541) 575-2873

Jerry Valdez
Valdez Silversmiths
R.R. 1, Box 62
Ft. Shaw, MT 59443
(406) 467-2044

Kelly Wardell
P.O. Box 258
Moorecroft, WY 82721
(307) 756-3668

Hitching and Braiding

The Ash Family
Rt. 1, Box 6C
Kooskia, ID 83539
(208) 926-0914

Casey Backus
Backus Braiding
5421 Frederick Dr.
Cheyenne, WY 82009
(307) 635-5985

Alfredo Campos
30028 Military Rd.
Federal Way, WA 98003
(206) 839-2205

Shoni and Ron Maulding
Hitching Tails
P.O. Box 1123
Kettle Falls, WA 99141
(509) 738-6944

Jeff Minor
Fine Custom Braidwork
606 Fulton
Salmon, ID 83467
(208) 756-4414

Lenny Spurlock
Hitched Horsehair
P.O. Box 1775
McCall, ID 83638
(208) 634-4947

Dealers

Big Bend Saddlery
P.O. Box 38
East Hwy 90
Alpine, TX 79831
(1-800) 634-4502, fax (915) 837-7278

Brighton Feed and Farm Supply Inc.
370 N. Main St.
Brighton, CO 80601
(1-800) 237-0721, (303) 659-0721

J. M. Capriola
500 Commercial St.
Elko, NV 89801
(702) 738-5816, fax (702) 738-8980

Double "H" Ranch and Feed Store
4230 Silverton Rd. N.E.
Salem, OR 97305
(1-800) 508-4973, (503) 362-4973,
fax (503) 362-3150

R. A. Gutherie Designs
P.O. Box 2438
Grass Valley, CA 95945
(916) 272-1533

Dave Hack
Custom Cowboy Gear
1915 N. 26th St.
Boise, ID 83702
(208) 343-5617

Hitching Post Supply
10312 — 210th St. S.E.
Snohomish, WA 98290
(360) 668-2349

Ray Holes Saddle Company
213 W. Main
Grangeville, ID 83530-1985
(208) 938-1460

King Saddlery
184 N. Main
Sheridan, WY 82801
(1-800) 443-8919, (307) 672-2702,
fax (307) 672-5235

Sagebrush Saddlery
1310 S. Ruby
Ellensburg, WA 98926
(509) 962-5282

Jeremiah Watt Products
Van Dyke Ranch
HC 1, Box 34
Coalinga, CA 93210
(209) 935-2172, fax (209) 935-1021